Where on Earth Am I?

ROBERT GARDNER

FRANKLIN WATTS
A Division of Grolier Publishing
New York—London—Hong Kong—Sydney
Danbury, Connecticut

ACKNOWLEDGMENTS

A special word of thanks to Carl Williams, former teaching colleague and long-time canoeist, who has spent most summers of his life leading canoe trips into the Canadian wilderness. The information, maps, and savvy comments he provided were extremely useful to me in preparing the manuscript for this book.

Photos copyright ©: Corbis-Bettman: 53, Courtesy of Magellan Systems: 146; Fundamental Phtos: 141; NASA: 14; Photo Researchers: 47 (NASA), 86 (Adam Hart-Davis/SPL), 134 (Richard T. Nowitz); Rolatape Measureing Systems: 69; U.S. Geological Survey: 98.

Library of Congress Cataloging-in-Publication Data

Gardner, Robert, 1929–
      Where on earth am I?/ by Robert Gardner.
            p.   cm.
      Includes bibliographical references and index.
      Summary: Offers a variety of investigations, activities, and projects explaining how humans discovered Earth's position in the universe, and how we can find our own location using maps, compasses, the sun, and the stars.
      ISBN 0-531-11297-7 (lib bdg.)   ISBN 0-531-15827-6 (pbk.)
      1. Earth—Juvenile literature. 2. Orientation—Juvenile literature.
[1. Earth. 2. Orientation.] I. Title.
QB631.4.G38 1996
526—dc20   96-12128
                                                                              CIP
                                                                              AC

Contents

Preface   7

Introduction   9

CHAPTER 1

The Shape of Our Planet   13

INVESTIGATION 1 Shapes and Shadows   15

Eratosthenes Measures the Earth   16

INVESTIGATION 2 Sun, Shadow, and Angle   17

The Earth's Imaginary Grid   18

INVESTIGATION 3 Angular Distances on the
   Celestial Sphere   20

INVESTIGATION 4 Which Eye Is Your Dominant Eye?   28

INVESTIGATION 5 Measuring the Girth of the Earth   28

Effects of the Earth's Curvature   32

CHAPTER 2

Who's Moving? 35

INVESTIGATION 6 Relative Motion 36
Two Points of View 36
INVESTIGATION 7 A Revolving Earth or a Revolving
Universe? 37
Copernicus, Galileo, and a New Model of the
Universe 38
ACTIVITY 1 Parallax 39
Galileo and the Lack of Parallax Among
the Stars 40
Acceptance of the Copernican Point of View 41
INVESTIGATION 8 How Far to the Planets? 42
Galileo, Venus, and the Copernican Model 46
The Orbital Radius of an Outer Planet 48
At Last! Parallax Among the Stars 51
How Can We Be Sure the Earth Is Rotating? 52
ACTIVITY 2 The Foucault Pendulum, a Model 55
Other Evidence of Earth's Rotation:
Coriolis Forces 56
ACTIVITY 3 The Coriolis Effect 58

CHAPTER 3

Measuring Distances on Earth 60

INVESTIGATION 9 Using Parallax to Measure Distance 61
INVESTIGATION 10 Finding Distance Using Similar
Triangles 65
INVESTIGATION 11 Finding Distance Using a
Range Finder 66
INVESTIGATION 12 Measuring Distance with Wheels 68
INVESTIGATION 13 Measuring Distance by Pacing 70
INVESTIGATION 14 Distance from Dead Reckoning 71
INVESTIGATION 15 Shortest Routes Along the Earth 73
Great Circle Routes 73

CHAPTER 4

Magnets, Compasses, and Directions 75

INVESTIGATION 16 Magnets and Magnetic Fields 75
Magnets, Compasses, and Magnetic Fields 76
INVESTIGATION 17 Finding Magnetic Declination
    Where You Live 82
INVESTIGATION 18 Electricity and Magnetism 83
INVESTIGATION 19 Making a Magnet
    and a Compass 84
The Orienteering Compass 85
INVESTIGATION 20 Finding Directions (Bearings) with an
    Orienteering Compass 88
ACTIVITY 4 Using a Compass to Follow a
    Direction (Bearing) 89
ACTIVITY 5 Using a Compass to Return to "Camp" 89
ACTIVITY 6 Using the Orienteering Compass to
    Walk a Triangle 90
ACTIVITY 7 Hiking Out and Back with an
    Orienteering Compass 92

CHAPTER 5

Maps and Mapping 96

Topographic Maps 97
INVESTIGATION 21 Mapping a Model Terrain 100
ACTIVITY 8 Mapping Hills 102
Mapping the World 107
INVESTIGATION 22 Finding Your Latitude 112
Finding Your Longitude 114
ACTIVITY 9 Mapping an Area of Land 115
ACTIVITY 10 Another Way to Make a Map 117
ACTIVITY 11 Using a Map 120
ACTIVITY 12 Travel by Map 121
ACTIVITY 13 Finding Landmarks 122

CHAPTER 6

Clues to Finding Your Way   124

INVESTIGATION 23 Can You Walk in a Straight Line?   125
Avoiding Curved Paths   126
Lost!   129
Estimating Distance   130

CHAPTER 7

Map, Compass, and Orienteering   133

ACTIVITY 14 Planning a Hike Using Map and Compass   133
ACTIVITY 15 Orienteering in Wilderness   136
ACTIVITY 16 Orienteering as a Sport   137

CHAPTER 8

Modern Methods of Finding Where on Earth You Are   139

Interference of Radio Waves   140
Loran   140
Global Positioning System (GPS)   142

APPENDIX

Where to Buy Maps   148

Glossary   150

For Further Reading   154

Index   155

Preface

The idea for this book came to me late one afternoon when, after riding my mountain bike into unfamiliar territory, I realized that I was lost. I mumbled, "Where on Earth am I?" At the same moment I thought, "That's a good title for a book!" As I looked around for directional clues such as the sun and the shadows cast by posts and trees, I began to think about ideas, activities, investigations, and projects that might provide the contents for the book you have just opened.

If I had been lost in the Canadian wilderness, far from civilization, I would probably have had different thoughts—thoughts of survival, not of a potential book—but being lost on the outer region of Cape Cod (north of the elbow) where I live is not life threatening. Since this strip of land that reaches out into the Atlantic Ocean is less than 3 kilometers (2 mi.) wide, I could have easily reached Cape Cod Bay by traveling west or the Atlantic Ocean by moving east. Consequently, becoming lost was an interesting and thought-provoking experience, not a frightening one.

By the time I had found a narrow trail leading westward and reached the Cape Cod Rail Trail, a relatively flat and very popular bicycle path that extends from Dennis to Wellfleet, I had prepared a rough outline of this book in my head. Upon arriving home, I went immediately to my office and put my thoughts into my computer's memory.

The book you are reading is the outcome of that experience, which I had about 5 years ago. The time from an idea to a book isn't always 5 years, but they are usually separated by a significant chunk of time—the time it takes to prepare a publishing proposal, find a publisher, write the book, and have it published.

Introduction

All of us carry mental maps that help us find our way in familiar territory. We navigate easily around our homes, schools, and towns because of maps etched in our brains. Upon entering a new school, it may take you a few days to develop an internal map that enables you to move quickly from one classroom to another or from gymnasium to auditorium to cafeteria. You can be sure that you possess such mental maps because you can draw them when you want to show others how to find their way around places familiar to you.

If you travel to an unknown city, a map helps you to find your way among unfamiliar streets and avenues, provided you have the map correctly oriented. However, if you haven't distinguished north from south, you may walk several blocks before you discover that you are moving in the wrong direction.

A road map is a valuable resource when driving through unfamiliar countryside, but again, you need to know north from south to avoid going in the wrong direction. A compass mounted on an automobile's dashboard is a useful addition to a map in helping drivers find their way through new territory. A traveler without a compass may turn to the stars or moon at night, or to the sun and the shadows it casts during the day for directional clues.

You have grown up watching Earth through the eyes of satellites. The view of our planet from space makes it clear that we live on the surface of a giant sphere. But people were not surprised when they first observed images of Earth from space. The shape of our globe, the outlines of the continents against the ocean waters that cover more than two-thirds of its surface, even its lakes and rivers were already known. Long before satellites were launched into space, before men walked on the moon, the shape of the Earth had been determined and accurate maps of its surface had been made.

For thousands of years, Earth was believed to be the center of the universe. Only during the last 350 years have people considered an alternative model, one that places us on a revolving, rotating planet that orbits the sun (together with eight other planets and an assortment of meteoroids, comets, and space debris). And, only during the last century have we come to accept the fact that Earth is but a tiny speck in a universe so vast as to tax our imaginations.

It was astronomers studying the stars and planets who suggested alternative models of Earth's place in the universe, and it was these same astronomers who used the star-filled heavens to map the Earth. By mapping the paths of the sun, moon, and stars as they moved across the sky, they learned to map our own planet and find their positions on it.

Today, we are able to navigate every part of the globe we inhabit, thanks to compasses that respond to Earth's magnetic field, maps based on aerial photographs and positions fixed by the stars, as well as very precise clocks. Atomic clocks on satellites and radio signals emitted by satellites make it possible for us to locate our position on the Earth's surface to within a few meters.

In this book you will conduct investigations that reveal how the shape and size of the Earth were determined thousands of years ago. You will learn, too, how its surface was mapped centuries before humans journeyed into space. Yet, despite our awareness of Earth's shape, the detailed maps of its surface, and our navigational technology, people still get lost and ask, "Where on Earth am I?" It's one thing to view Earth from afar; it's quite another to view it from a bramble patch surrounded by trees or swampland, from the middle of an ocean, or from an airplane above arctic tundra. We learn all too well that the adage "You can't see the forest for the trees!" applies in the literal as well as the figurative sense. By learning how to use maps, compasses, and clues that keep you on a straight-line path, you will learn to avoid becoming lost and come to enjoy the excitement of finding your way in the great outdoors. You will learn to know where on Earth you are—and how to move from where you are to where you want to be.

CHAPTER 1

The Shape of Our Planet

Locating our position on Earth is complicated by the fact that we live on a sphere, a sphere so large that it appears flat to anyone standing on its surface. Even young children will tell you that the Earth is round, and every adult knows that the Earth is a sphere, but how did people discover that we live on a globe?

Photographs of Earth taken from space or from the moon's surface provide convincing evidence of Earth's shape, but these photographs did not surprise anyone. People have known for centuries that we live on a globe. Yet, if you look out across the plains of Kansas or the oceans from points along the East and West Coasts of the United States, the Earth appears to be flat. If you were a sailor in ancient times, you might have avoided sailing beyond sight of land for fear you would fall off the edge of a disk-shaped earth. How did early astronomers and geographers determine the shape of the Earth?

Aristotle (384–322 B.C.), a famous Greek philosopher, may have been the first to offer evidence that the Earth is a sphere. He noticed that during an eclipse of the moon, the edge of the Earth's shadow seen on the lunar surface is always curved. Only a sphere casts a shadow that is always curved. Aristotle also found that for northbound travelers hitherto unseen stars appeared on the northern horizon, while stars on the southern horizon disappeared. The opposite was true for southbound travelers. The effect could easily be explained if the Earth is spherical.

On clear, dry days, people looking to the horizon across the ocean in anticipation of a returning ship saw the ship's mast and sails come into view before its hull. A curved Earth would explain why the taller structures of a ship appeared first as it approached land.

INVESTIGATION

Shapes and Shadows

Aristotle argued that the Earth is a sphere because the edge of its shadow, which appeared on the moon during an eclipse, is always curved. Only a sphere, he maintained, would *always* cast a round shadow. Is this true?

To find out, place a single light bulb near one side of an otherwise dark room. The bulb will be used to cast shadows of objects placed near a light-colored wall on the opposite side of the room. The wall will serve as a screen for shadows.

Begin with a sphere such as a ball or an orange. Hold the

This photo, taken from Apollo 17 on its trip to the moon, certainly reveals Earth's spherical shape. The white area at the bottom is the polar ice cap in Antarctica. Can you identify the continent that lies above it?

sphere near the wall and turn it in various ways. Does the sphere always cast a round shadow?

Are there other shapes that will always cast round shadows? To find out, repeat the experiment with a disk-shaped object such as the top of a can or a Frisbee®. Can you hold the disk so that it casts a round shadow? Can the disk cast shadows that are not round? If so, how many different shadow shapes can it cast?

Use a cylinder, such as a tin can, to cast shadows. Can a cylinder cast a round shadow? Can it cast shadows with other shapes? If so, how many different shadow shapes can it cast?

If possible, use a cone to cast shadows. Can a cone cast a round shadow? Can it cast shadows with other shapes? If so, how many different shadows can it cast? What other objects might cast round shadows? Do these objects *always* cast a round shadow?

Eratosthenes Measures the Earth

Eratosthenes (276–196 B.C.), curator of the world's first major library and museum in Alexandria, Egypt, was probably the first person to measure the Earth's diameter. He did it by measuring a shadow. Eratosthenes knew that at midday on the summer solstice (about June 20 on modern calendars) the sun's image could be seen in a deep well in Syene, a city 500 miles south of Alexandria.* This meant that the sun must be directly over Syene at that time.

On one such summer solstice, Eratosthenes measured the shadow of a tall tower in Alexandria at midday. He found

---

* Throughout this book, some measurements are given only in metric or English units. This is because it is important for you to know that measurement's value precisely. Whenever a value is converted from metric to English units (or vice versa), a degree of accuracy is lost when the value is rounded to the nearest significant figure.

16

that the ratio of the tower's height to its shadow's length was 15:2.

Sun, Shadow, and Angle

If you know basic trigonometry, you can determine the angle that the sun's rays made with the top of the tower in Alexandria using the ratio of the tower's height to the shadow's length. If you have no knowledge of trigonometry, you can still determine the angle. Simply draw a vertical line exactly 15 centimeters long to represent the tower. Then, at the base of the vertical line draw a horizontal line exactly 2 centimeters long to represent the tower's shadow. Finally, draw a line connecting the tip of the "shadow" with the top of the "tower." This line represents a ray of sunlight that just skims the top of the tower and defines the end of the shadow. Use a *protractor* to measure the angle that the sun's rays make with the tower and the ground.

From Investigation 2, you probably found, as did Eratosthenes, that moving 500 miles north of Syene changed the angle of the sun's rays by 7.6° (from 90° to 82.4°). Eratosthenes realized that the change in the angle at which the sun's light struck the Earth was a result of the Earth's curvature. He reasoned that, if the angle changed by 7.6° over 500 miles, he could determine the distance needed to change it by 360°. By letting X represent the Earth's circumference, he solved an equation like the one below.

$$500 \text{ mi.}/7.6° = X/360°$$
$$X = (500 \text{ mi.}/7.6°)(360°) = 23,700 \text{ mi.}$$

His calculation gave a result that was within 5 percent of the Earth's actual circumference. However, most scholars at that time didn't believe the Earth was that large and they ignored his work.

The Earth's Imaginary Grid

A *great circle* is any circle on the surface of a sphere in which the center is at the center of the sphere. The Earth's equator is a great circle. We can also imagine a series of great circles with circumferences that pass through the Earth's poles. These circles, which intersect the equator at right angles, are called *meridians*. They are like the lines you find separating the sections of a peeled orange.

You will find these meridians on a map or a globe; you will also find lines that are drawn parallel to Earth's equator. These are lines of *latitude*—imaginary lines that go east-west around the Earth (Figure 1). The line of latitude that goes around the equator is defined as the 0° line. The North Pole is at 90° north; the South Pole is at 90° south. Between the equator and the poles are lines of latitude that divide the Northern and Southern Hemispheres into equally spaced degrees extending from 0° to 90°.

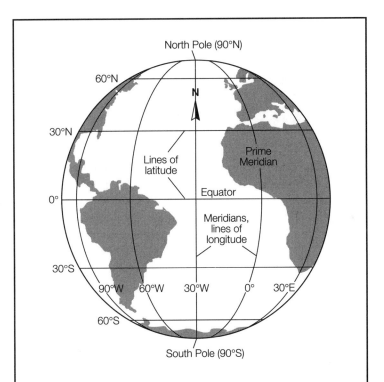

Figure 1 Lines of latitude and longitude are used to divide the Earth into degrees. Lines of latitude run east to west (parallel to the equator). Lines of longitude run north to south. They extend from the Prime Meridian (0°), which passes through Greenwich, England, westward to 180°W or eastward to 180°E.

Meridians divide Earth's surface into segments east or west of an arbitrary meridian defined as 0°. These lines, often called lines of *longitude*, are found on maps and globes. The line that passes through Greenwich, England, called the *Prime Meridian*, was established in 1884 by a worldwide agreement. It is defined as 0° longitude. Other meridians east and west of Greenwich divide the Earth into two hemispheres. The Western Hemisphere extends 180° west of Greenwich; the Eastern Hemisphere extends 180° east of Greenwich. Together, the two hemispheres make up the spherical Earth's 360°.

Early astronomers believed that Earth was at the center of a huge celestial sphere (the sky) that rotated about Earth. To make their model of the universe as simple as possible, they placed the celestial sphere's equator on the same plane as Earth's equator. Similarly, the celestial poles were located directly above Earth's poles, as shown in Figure 2. Astronomers and others still find the idea of a celestial sphere useful, even though they know that the sphere doesn't really rotate about the Earth.

INVESTIGATION 3

Angular Distances on the Celestial Sphere

Early astronomers knew that the diameter of the celestial sphere was large, but they had no idea how large it was. Present-day astronomers know that there is no fixed value for the diameter of the celestial sphere. Even though the stars appear to glimmer on the surface of a sphere, their distances from Earth are vastly different. The distance to the nearest star is 4.3 light-years—more than 40 trillion kilometers (25 trillion mi.)—and the distances to other stars are much, much greater. Consequently, for both ancient and modern astronomers it was, and still is, convenient to measure the separation of stars in terms of angles on the celestial sphere. For example, the angular separation between a star that is directly overhead and one that is on the horizon is 90°.

You can build a simple device to make angular measurements on the celestial sphere. You know that a circle contains 360°. Now imagine a circle with a 360-centimeter circumference, as shown in Figure 3. Each centimeter on the circumference of such a circle would be 1° wide when viewed along a radius of the circle; a 10-centimeter portion of the circumfer-

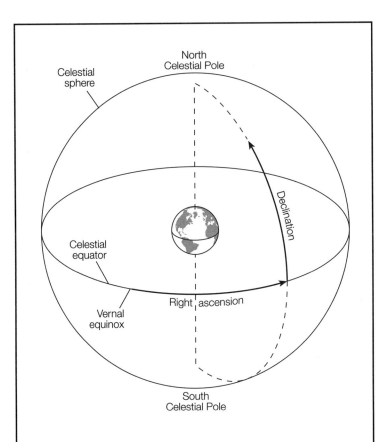

Figure 2 The poles and equator of the celestial sphere are extensions of the Earth's poles and equator. However, longitude on the celestial sphere is called right ascension and declination is used in place of latitude. Right ascension is measured in units of time (hours, minutes, seconds) eastward along the celestial equator starting at the vernal equinox—the point where the sun crosses the equator as it moves northward, a point in time that marks the beginning of spring. Declination is the angle (measured in degrees, minutes, and seconds) north or south of the equator.

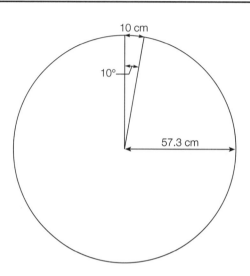

Figure 3 For a circle with a circumference of 360 centimeters, each centimeter subtends one degree. Ten centimeters of circumference subtends 10°, 20 centimeters subtends 20°, etc. The radius of such a circle is 57.3 centimeters.

ence would be seen as 10° from the circle's center. Since the circumference (C) of a circle is equal to the circle's radius (r) multiplied by 2π, the radius of a circle with a circumference of 360 centimeters is 57.3 centimeters because

$$r = C/2\pi = 360 \text{ cm}/2\pi = 57.3 \text{ cm.}$$

You can use that information to build a device that will allow you to make angular measurements on the celestial sphere. Cut a 4 inch × 6 inch (10 cm × 15 cm) file card in half as shown in Figure 4a. Then cut out sections that are each 1 cm wide and 1, 2, 5, and 10 centimeters long. See Figure 4b. Tape the card 57.3 centimeters from one end of a meter stick as shown in Figure 4c. Or you can cut a stick so that it is 57.3 centimeters

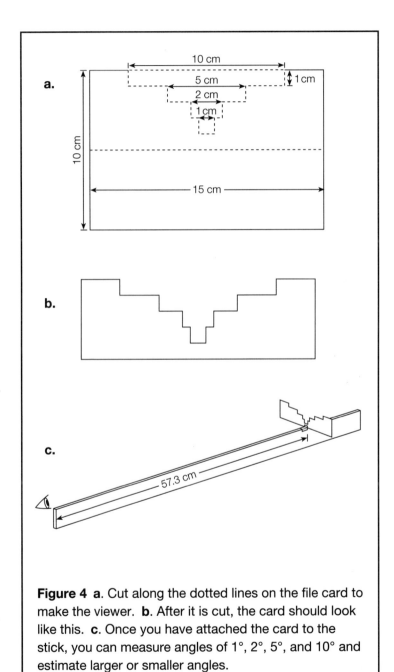

Figure 4 a. Cut along the dotted lines on the file card to make the viewer. **b.** After it is cut, the card should look like this. **c.** Once you have attached the card to the stick, you can measure angles of 1°, 2°, 5°, and 10° and estimate larger or smaller angles.

long and tape the card to its end. By placing your eye at the opposite end of the stick, you will be able to look through the gaps in the card and estimate the angular separations of stars, planets, and moon on the celestial hemisphere. For example, if two stars are at the edges of the 2-centimeter slot, their separation is 2°.

Find a dark location where you can use your device to make angular measurements on the celestial sphere. DO NOT LOOK AT THE SUN. IT CAN DAMAGE YOUR EYES. If the moon is visible, measure the angular diameter of the moon. What angle does the moon's diameter *subtend* (cover)?

Find the Big Dipper in the northern sky (Figure 5). It turns about the Earth's North Pole like the tip of a clock's hand, so you may find it at a variety of positions, depending on season and time. What is the angular width of the Big Dipper, including its bowl and handle?

Find the two stars at the end of the Dipper bowl (Merak and Dubhe). What angle is subtended by their separation? Merak and Dubhe are called the pointer stars. If you continue along the imaginary line between Merak and Dubhe, you will come to a point very near the North Star (Polaris). Polaris is the star at the end of the handle of the Little Dipper, a constellation significantly dimmer than the Big Dipper. The distance from Dubhe to Polaris is a little more than five times the distance from Merak to Dubhe. How many degrees should that be? Measure that angle outward from Dubhe along the line on the celestial sphere established by Merak and Dubhe. You will find Polaris just beyond the end of that line. Polaris is at the end of the handle of the Little Dipper. What is the angular width of the Little Dipper, including its bowl and handle?

What is the angular width of the Big Dipper's handle? Alkaid is the name of the star at the end of the handle. When Alkaid is directly above or below Polaris, Polaris is at true north (exactly over the North Pole).

There is no star directly over the Earth's South Pole. However, the four stars of the Southern Cross (Crux) together with

24

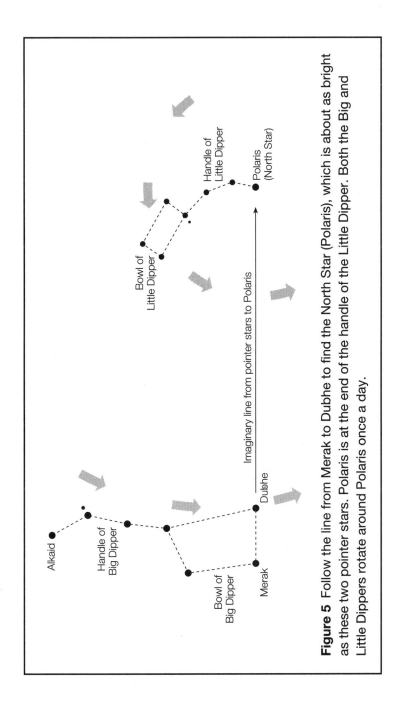

Figure 5 Follow the line from Merak to Dubhe to find the North Star (Polaris), which is about as bright as these two pointer stars. Polaris is at the end of the handle of the Little Dipper. Both the Big and Little Dippers rotate around Polaris once a day.

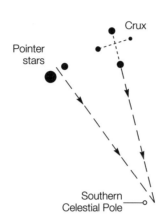

Figure 6 In the Southern Hemisphere, the Southern Cross (Crux) and the two nearby bright pointer stars will guide your eyes to a point that is close to the Southern Celestial Pole, which is directly over the Earth's South Pole.

two bright pointer stars nearby can locate a point close to the Southern Celestial Pole. Follow the lines established by the Southern Cross and the pointers to the point where they intersect, as shown in Figure 6.

Figure 7 shows a few of the brightest and most familiar constellations found in the night sky at different times of the year. Look for some of these and other constellations in the sky and measure the angles they subtend. Notice that Cassiopeia, which lies on the opposite side of Polaris from the Big Dipper, and Cepheus (as well as the Big Dipper and Little Dipper) are visible most of the year in much of the United States and Canada. Such constellations are called circumpolar constellations. They lie so close to Polaris that they never set when viewed from much of the Northern Hemisphere.

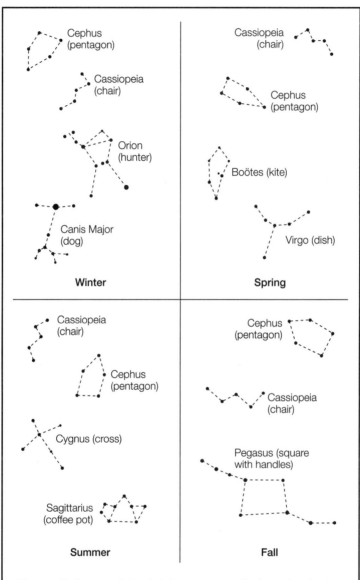

Winter

Cephus (pentagon)

Cassiopeia (chair)

Orion (hunter)

Canis Major (dog)

Spring

Cassiopeia (chair)

Cephus (pentagon)

Boötes (kite)

Virgo (dish)

Summer

Cassiopeia (chair)

Cephus (pentagon)

Cygnus (cross)

Sagittarius (coffee pot)

Fall

Cephus (pentagon)

Cassiopeia (chair)

Pegasus (square with handles)

Figure 7 Some of the brightest constellations (and what you may think they resemble) seen in the night sky during different seasons.

PROJECT 3

The speed of light is 300,000 kilometers per second (3.0×10^5 km/s) or 186,000 miles per second (1.9×10^5 mi./s). Using this velocity, show that the nearest star, which is 4.3 light-years away, is more than 40 trillion kilometers (25 trillion mi.) from us.

INVESTIGATION 4

Which Eye Is Your Dominant Eye?

To find positions on Earth, you have to establish *sightlines*. In the next investigation, for example, you will be asked to make a sightline to the North Star. To do this correctly, you should use your dominant eye. But which of your eyes is dominant?

To find out, extend your arm with your thumb in a "thumbs up" gesture. Keeping both eyes open, align your thumb with a distant object such as a post or pole. Now close first one eye and then the other. In one case, your thumb and the object will remain aligned; with the other eye, your thumb and the object will no longer lie along a line connecting your eye with the distant object. The eye that remains aligned with the distant object is your dominant eye.

INVESTIGATION 5

Measuring the Girth of the Earth

To make your own estimate of the Earth's circumference and diameter, you will need a globe with a diameter of about 30 centimeters (12 in.), a large empty can or other suitable base for the globe, a cloth measuring tape or flexible ruler, a common pin, a piece of clay, and a drinking straw. You will also need to establish a north–south line, which you can do by watching the shadow of a vertical post or stick near midday. Try to do this experiment between the first of April and the middle of September where the sun's path across the Earth is above the equator.

Mark the end of the shadow of the vertical post or stick at frequent intervals near midday. Be aware that midday, the time when the sun is highest in the sky, may not occur at noon. The post's or stick's shadow will be shortest at midday (when the sun is due south) if you are at a latitude greater than 23.5°N. If you draw a line between the center of the post or stick and the end of its shortest shadow, you will have a north–south line.

Alternatively, you can mark the end of the vertical stick's shadow a few minutes before midday. Then, use a string and a stick to make a semicircle on the ground around the stick. (The radius of the circle should match the length of the shadow.) The shadow will move from west to east inside the circumference of the semicircle you drew.

Mark the point where the stick's shadow again touches the circumference. Draw a straight line between the two points where the shadow touched the circumference. A line drawn from the stick to the midpoint of the first line will indicate true north.

After nightfall, you might like to compare your true-north line with a sightline to Polaris. The sightline to the star should lie directly or almost directly above the north–south line you made using the stick and its shadow.

Place the globe on a large empty can or other suitable support. Turn the globe so it represents the way you see the Earth—so that the point representing your location on the globe is uppermost. Use a pin supported by a small piece of clay to represent your location on the globe. With your town at the top of the globe, turn it so that the globe's axis is along the north–south line you have made. Why will the globe's North Pole now point toward Polaris? (See Figure 8.)

Study the globe and the shadows you see on it carefully. Where on Earth is the sun rising at this moment? Where on Earth is the sun setting? Which continents and cities are in darkness? Are there places near either pole where the sun will

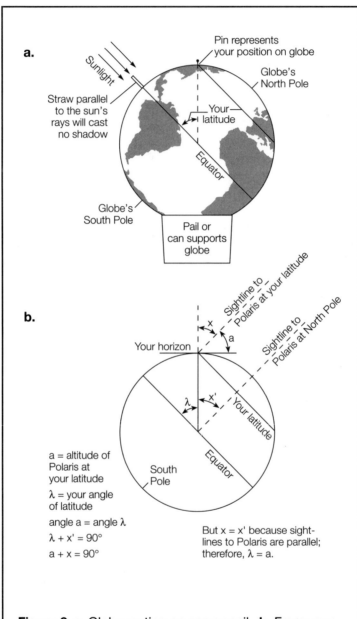

Figure 8 a. Globe resting on can or pail. **b.** From your latitude, Polaris is at angle a above your horizon.

shine all day? Are there places near a pole where the sun will not shine at all today?

Since a perpendicular stick will not cast a shadow when the sun is directly above it, you can now locate your "Syene" (the place on Earth where the sun is directly overhead at this moment). Use a short piece of a drinking straw to represent the deep well at Syene. Stick a pin through the straw and move along the globe's surface (the straw should be perpendicular to the globe) until you find a place where the sun shines straight down through the straw and, therefore, casts no shadow. Note the latitude of the place where the sun is directly overhead at this moment. If your globe is correctly oriented, the sun will continue to move along this latitude throughout the day.

Use a cloth measuring tape or a flexible ruler to measure the north–south distance between the latitude of your location on the globe and the latitude where the sun is directly overhead. Next, measure the midday shadow of the vertical stick you used before. What is the ratio of the length of the shadow to the height of the stick?

Use that ratio to determine the angle that the sun makes with the stick. (See Investigation 2.) Then use that angle and the distance on the globe between the latitude of your location and the latitude where the sun is directly overhead to predict the circumference of the globe you are using.

How does your prediction compare with the actual circumference of that globe? What is the globe's diameter according to your calculations?

The distance from one degree of latitude to the next is 111 kilometers, 69 miles, or 60 nautical miles. Use your experimental information to determine the circumference and diameter of the Earth in kilometers, miles, and nautical miles.

PROJECT 4

Earth's circumference is 21,600 nautical miles. Show that one nautical mile north or south along a line of latitude is equivalent to 1 minute of latitude. Where on Earth would 1 nautical mile be equivalent to 1 minute of *longitude*?

PROJECT 5

Many political issues involve latitude or longitude. In 1844, the Democratic Party used the phrase, "Fifty-four forty or fight," as a campaign slogan. What was the significance of that slogan? What other issues involving latitude or longitude can you find in U.S. history?

Effects of the Earth's Curvature

Because the Earth is spherical, its surface curves away from us regardless of where we stand. The limit of our visibility is called our *horizon*, but the distance to our horizon varies. As you can see from Figure 9a, the higher (h) your view, the greater the distance (d) you can see across the Earth's surface. Also, from Figure 9b, you can see that the greater the height of the object (h), the greater the distance (d) that its top can be seen projecting above the horizon. In either case, as the equations show, since the height is so small compared to the radius (r) of the Earth, h^2 would be insignificant in solving the Pythagorean equation, and so solving for h we find that $h = d^2/2r$.

Using the equation, you can see that over a distance of 1 mile the horizon drops away from our line of sight by an amount that can be calculated. Since the radius of the Earth, r, is very nearly 4,000 miles, the drop of the horizon at a distance (d) of 1 mile is easily calculated:

$$h = d^2/2r = (1 \text{ mi.})^2/(2 \times 4{,}000 \text{ mi.}) = 0.000125 \text{ mi.}$$

Since there are 5,280 feet in a mile, the drop of the horizon in feet is

$$0.000125 \text{ mi.} \times 5{,}280 \text{ ft./mi.} = 0.66 \text{ ft.}$$

32

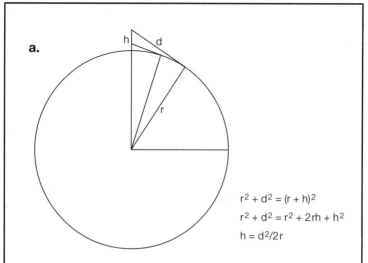

a.

$$r^2 + d^2 = (r + h)^2$$
$$r^2 + d^2 = r^2 + 2rh + h^2$$
$$h = d^2/2r$$

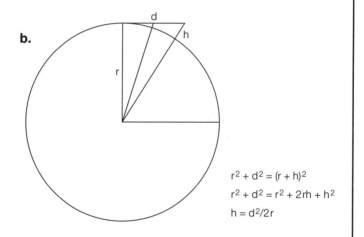

b.

$$r^2 + d^2 = (r + h)^2$$
$$r^2 + d^2 = r^2 + 2rh + h^2$$
$$h = d^2/2r$$

Figure 9 a. The distance (d) to the horizon increases as your height (h) above the earth increases.
b. The taller the object, the greater the distance that it can be seen across the surface of a spherical Earth.

PROJECT 6

Show that the horizon will drop away from your line of sight by 2.64 feet over a distance of 2 miles and by 5.94 feet over a distance of 3 miles.

PROJECT 7

Can a person who is 6 feet tall see people across a lake 4 miles wide?

PROJECT 8

Early sailors in the Mediterranean Sea used high mountains as sight points. Over what distance could a mountain 8,000 feet high be seen?

CHAPTER 2

Who's Moving?

One way to find your position on Earth is to read the maps found in the sky. Each day we see the sun rise in the east and set in the west. The moon, stars, and planets follow similar paths across the sky each day. The stars that make up the eighty-eight constellations that cross the celestial dome, such as the Big Dipper, Orion, Sagittarius, and Boötes, form recognizable configurations that do not change position relative to one another. For this reason, they are called the fixed stars.

It was obvious to early observers that the sun and moon move relative to one another and to the fixed stars. The moon passes in front of a dozen constellations each month, and the sun makes a similar number of passings each year. But other celestial objects, originally thought to be stars, also seemed to shift relative to the fixed stars. These bodies were called "wanderers" because their positions in the sky shifted, but more slowly than those of the sun and moon. Later it was discovered that they were planets (Mercury, Venus,

Mars, Jupiter, and Saturn), each revolving at its own rate about the sun. The other planets in the solar system—Uranus, Neptune, and Pluto—were not discovered until the eighteenth, nineteenth, and twentieth centuries respectively.

We say these celestial bodies "move" across the sky, and, indeed, that is what they appear to do. But what is "moving?" Do the celestial bodies move about us, or does the Earth turn, causing the sun, moon, planets, and stars to *appear* to move in circular paths around us?

INVESTIGATION 6

Relative Motion

Stand in a dark room, and let your head represent the Earth. Assume that east is to your left and west is to your right. Ask someone to turn on a flashlight, which represents the sun, and keep it pointed at your head while slowly walking around you from your left to your right (east to west). In which direction do you see the "sun" rise? In which direction does it set?

Now ask the same person to stand to your left with the flashlight pointed at your head. Then turn slowly to your left (east). In which direction does the "sun" rise? In which direction does the sun set?

Two Points of View

For centuries, people assumed that celestial bodies move from east to west about the Earth, an Earth that was the center of the universe. After all, they argued, objects fall toward the Earth, and Earth is inhabited by humans who were created in God's image. However, in 1543, shortly before his death, the Polish astronomer Nicolas Copernicus published *De Revolutionibus Orbium Celestium* (*On the Revolutions of the Celestial Spheres*). He suggested that the motion of the celestial bodies could be explained if the Earth rotates from west to east on an axis that runs through its poles.

As you saw in Investigation 6, the sun appears to rise in the east and set in the west regardless of whether the sun moves from east to west or the Earth turns from west to east. The observed motion of celestial bodies is the same from either frame of reference.

Copernicus's model extended further. He reasoned that just as the Earth might rotate on its axis once each day, so might it revolve about the sun once each year. Indeed, he suggested that we might live in a *heliocentric* (sun-centered) solar system in which all the planets revolve slowly about the sun, rather than in a *geocentric* (Earth-centered) universe where all celestial bodies speed rapidly around the Earth each day.

INVESTIGATION 7

A Revolving Earth or a Revolving Universe?

Place twelve chairs or other objects in a circle around the periphery of a large room. The chairs or other objects represent the twelve constellations through which the sun moves each year. These are the constellations of the zodiac—Aries, Taurus, Gemini, Cancer, Leo, Virgo, Libra, Scorpio, Sagittarius, Capricorn, Aquarius, and Pisces. Darken the room and stand in the center. Again, let your head represent the Earth. Ask someone to hold a flashlight, which represents the sun. Ideally, in a geocentric model, the chairs (constellations of the zodiac) would move about you once a day, as on a merry-go-round, while the person holding the flashlight (sun) walks very, very slowly along the moving merry-go-round in front of the constellations. By the time the "sun" had made 365 "orbits" around you, it would have moved in front of each of the constellations and back to its original position on the merry-go-round.

Since you probably don't have a merry-go-round or a giant lazy Susan, you will have to imagine that the "constellations" are moving about you very nearly as fast as the person holding the flashlight. Each orbit of the flashlight about your head represents one day.

To make a heliocentric model, place a single light bulb, representing the sun, at the center of the room. Walk very slowly around the light bulb. Your moving head represents the Earth's path around the sun. Of course, you should be rotating as you revolve around the light bulb, but to avoid becoming dizzy, stop and turn around slowly so as to represent the Earth's rotation during a single day. As you face the light bulb (sun), you will see that it lies in front of a particular chair (constellation), such as Sagittarius. Astronomers would say the sun is *in* Sagittarius. When you turn another 180° so that it is "midnight," you will see the constellation where the sun will be located half an orbit from now (6 months in real time).

Now, move another half orbit around the sun. Face the sun and you will see that the sun is now in the constellation that was in your midnight sky on your earlier stop. Turn 180° to change day to night and you will see the constellation that was behind the sun on the other side of the orbit.

How does your model explain why we see a different pattern of stars in the sky as we move from one season to the next?

Copernicus, Galileo, and a New Model of the Universe

As you found in Investigation 7, Copernicus's explanation of the sun's movement along the zodiac (using a heliocentric model) was just as satisfactory as the traditional geocentric model of the universe. Nevertheless, few accepted the Copernican model. Copernicus probably delayed publishing his ideas as long as possible because he realized he would be branded a heretic. It was Galileo who took the brunt of the criticism more than half a century later when he endorsed the Copernican view.

Through the telescope he had built, Galileo was able to see the imperfections on the surface of the moon—its mountains and seas. Images of the sun formed by the lenses in his telescope were focused on a screen revealing that the sun, too, was imperfect. It contained dark areas (sunspots) that changed with time. Yet, like all celestial bodies, the sun and moon were supposed to be perfectly uniform and unchanging.

Galileo also detected four of Jupiter's moons. By watching them night after night, it was clear to him that these moons revolved about the planet. Despite accepted dogma, here was *evidence* that not every celestial body revolved about the Earth. If moons could revolve about Jupiter, then surely the Earth could revolve about the sun. To those who objected by saying that a rotating Earth would fly apart, Galileo responded with the words of Copernicus, "Why does the defender of the geocentric theory not fear the same fate for his rotating celestial sphere—so much faster because so much larger?"

For those who reasoned that birds and clouds would be left behind by a rotating Earth, Galileo argued that the atmosphere was a part of the Earth and rotated at the same rate. But if the Earth revolves around the sun, why do the stars, which are quite likely at different distances from Earth, show no *parallax*; that is, why do the stars not appear to change position relative to one another as the Earth moves from one side of its orbit to the other?

ACTIVITY

Parallax

You can observe parallax using your eyes and fingers. Consider your two eyes to be opposite ends of a base line from which objects are viewed. (On a much larger scale, the opposite sides of the Earth's orbit could represent a base line for viewing the stars.) Hold your two index fingers upright in front of your face. Hold one finger about a foot away; hold the other at arm's length. Close one eye. Use the open eye to line up the two fingers with a distant object. Now shift to the opposite end of the base line by closing the eye you had used to form a sight-line and opening the other eye. You will find that the two fingers are no longer aligned and neither finger is in line with the distant object. Next, hold one finger on top of the other. When you view them first with one eye and then with the other, they do not shift relative to one another because they are both at the same place and the same distance from your eyes. They do, however, shift with respect to more distant objects. This shifting of two objects relative to one another when viewed from different ends of a base line is called parallax.

Galileo and the Lack of Parallax Among the Stars

At the time of Copernicus and Galileo, no one had been able to detect any parallax among the stars when viewed at different times of the year. This fact was used as evidence that the Earth did not move. If it did, then the near stars should shift position relative to the more distant ones. Galileo argued that the distance to even the nearest star was so much greater than the diameter of the Earth's orbit that the parallax could not be detected.

PROJECT 9

The diameter of the Earth's orbit is very nearly 300 million kilometers (3.0×10^8 km) or 190 million miles (1.9×10^8 mi.). The nearest star (Alpha Centauri) is approximately 4.3 light-years away. A light-year is the distance light travels in 1 year or 31,557,600 seconds. Since light travels at 300,000 kilometers per second (186,000 mi./s), what distance is equivalent to one light-year? To 4.3 light-years? What is the ratio of the distance between Earth and Alpha Centauri to the diameter of the Earth's orbit? Through what angle would Alpha Centauri appear to shift when viewed from opposite ends of Earth's orbit? Was Galileo correct in assuming that stars were too distant for parallax to be detected? Someone has said that the Earth's orbit as seen from a near star would be like looking at a quarter from a distance of 3 km (2 mi.). Does this statement agree with what you have calculated for the ratio of the distance to Alpha Centauri to the diameter of the Earth's orbit?

Acceptance of the Copernican Point of View

Although the Roman Catholic Church forced Galileo to recant his Copernican views in his later years, the evidence he and others accumulated was too compelling to be denied.

One of those who added evidence to the Copernican model was German astronomer Johannes Kepler (1571–1630). Using the astronomical data gathered by Danish astronomer Tycho Brahe (1546–1601) in his painstaking measurements of the positions of the planets and stars, Kepler was able to show that planets travel along elliptical orbits as they move about the sun, and that an imaginary line connecting a planet with the sun sweeps out equal areas in equal periods of time (Figure 10). Using the vast data collected by Brahe, Kepler concluded that the ratio of the cube of a planet's radius to the square of its *period* is the same for all the planets in the solar system. Mathematically, this relationship can be written as $R^3/T^2 = K$.

By the time Isaac Newton published his laws of motion and gravitation in 1687, few scientists doubted that we live on a planet that orbits the sun along with all the other planets in this solar system. However, concrete evidence that the Earth truly does move was not found until the 1800s.

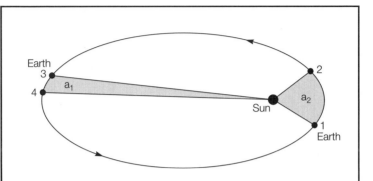

Figure 10 The times required for the Earth to move from position 1 to position 2 and from position 3 to position 4 are equal. During those equal times, the areas a_1 and a_2 swept out by a line connecting the Earth and the sun are equal. Although Earth's orbit is almost perfectly circular, a very elliptical orbit has been shown here to illustrate Kepler's law. This drawing is not to scale.

PROJECT 10

Using the data given in Table 1, show that R^3/T^2 is a constant, and find the value of that constant. (Kepler thought that six planets orbited the sun. Uranus, Neptune, and Pluto were not observed until more recently.)

INVESTIGATION 8

How Far to the Planets?

Kepler and other astronomers used a variety of methods to find the distances to planets moving along their orbits around the sun. In this investigation you will measure the radius of the orbit of Venus, a planet inside Earth's orbit. Later you will read about

Table 1: Orbital Radii and Periods of the Planets

Name of planet	Radius of orbit (AU)*	Period (years)**
Mercury	0.389	0.241
Venus	0.723	0.614
Earth	1.00	1.00
Mars	1.53	1.88
Jupiter	5.22	11.8
Saturn	9.60	29.4
Uranus	19.3	84.7
Neptune	30.2	165
Pluto	39.6	247

* The radii are in astronomical units (AU). One AU is the distance of Earth from the sun.

** The periods are given in fractions or multiples of one Earth year.

one way to find the orbital radius of a planet that lies outside Earth's orbit. Both radii will be measured in terms of the *astronomical unit* (AU)—the radius of Earth's orbit.

From Figure 11, you can see that angle VES is greatest when a line connecting Venus and Earth is tangent to the orbit of Venus, an orbit that is very nearly a circle. At this point the angle SVE formed by the lines connecting Venus with the sun and with Earth is a right angle because, as a geometric theorem proves, a tangent to a circle is perpendicular to a radius drawn to the tangent.

Since Venus is usually visible near the sun as a morning or evening "star," you can measure the angle VES at its maximum value quite easily. All that's required is the patience to wait until the separation between Venus and the sun reaches a maximum. Try to find Venus just before sunrise or sunset. It is the brightest object in the sky (except for the sun and moon) so it should not be hard to find against a dimming sky. *The Old Farmer's Almanac* or a newspaper will help you to determine

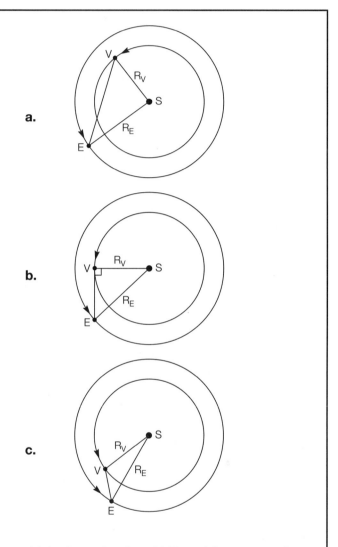

a.

b.

c.

Figure 11 In these drawings V, E, and S represent the positions of Venus, Earth, and the sun respectively. R_E is the radius of Earth's orbit; R_V is the radius of Venus's orbit. Angle VES is at its maximum in drawing (**b**) when the line VE connecting Venus and Earth is tangent to Venus's orbit.

the time of sunrise or sunset, whether or not Venus is visible, and whether it is a morning or evening star.

To find the angle between the sun and Venus, use the device you made for Investigation 3 to measure angular distances on the celestial sphere. As Venus slowly approaches and reaches its maximum angle from the sun (which may take months), the separation will be considerably more than 10°. Consequently, you will either have to use a larger card or move the stick and card several times to find the angular separation.

As shown in Figure 12, you can also make a rough measurement by finding how many of your fists at arm's length separate the rising or setting sun and Venus. A fist at arm's length

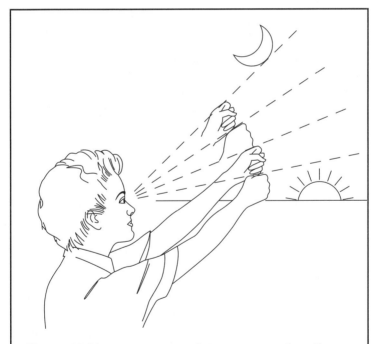

Figure 12 You can use your fists, one upon the other, upon the other . . . to estimate angles along the celestial hemisphere. One fist at arm's length is approximately 10° of arc.

covers about 10° of arc. Use the edge of the sun as it rises or sets as a base line for your measurement. DO NOT LOOK DIRECTLY AT THE SUN. IT CAN DAMAGE YOUR EYES.

What is the largest angle (VES in Figure 11) that you can observe between Venus and the sun? Using that maximum angle, determine the radius of the orbit of Venus in astronomical units (AU). You can use your knowledge of trigonometry or make a scale drawing using a ruler, pencil, and protractor. How does your value compare with the one given in Table 1? According to the orbital radius in Table 1, what should be the maximum angular separation between Venus and the sun as seen from Earth? How does it compare with your value?

If you have binoculars or a small telescope, you will enjoy watching Venus over a period of months. What do you notice about the planet's shape? Does it go through phases much like the moon?

PROJECT 11

Early in the 1500s, Copernicus estimated that the largest angle between the sun and Mercury was 22.3°. Based on this, what is the radius of Mercury's orbit in AU? How does that value compare with the one given in Table 1?

Galileo, Venus, and the Copernican Model

During the hours of twilight and dawn when, perhaps like you, Galileo focused his telescope on Venus day after day and month after month, he discovered that the planet appeared to change its shape. It went through phases, much like the phases of the moon that we see each month. His observations convinced him that Venus must orbit the sun.

Astronomers had known for centuries that Venus never strayed more than 47° from the sun. Although Greek as-

March 15, 1967

April 26, 1967

May 5, 1967

May 22, 1967

June 13, 1967

July 26, 1967

These photos of Venus were taken between March 15 and July 26 of 1967. They show the changing size and shape of the planet as seen from Earth.

tronomers living as early as Ptolemy (127-151) had been able to come up with possible explanations for why Venus stayed close to the sun, Galileo realized that the phases that he observed with his telescope could be explained only if Venus orbited the sun. This is made clear by Figure 13. Galileo noted, too, that Venus appeared smallest when its phase was full, and largest when it was new or a crescent. This finding fit the heliocentric model. When Venus was full, it would be on the far side of the sun and farthest from Earth. Thus, it would appear smallest when full and largest when new or a crescent. As you can see from the photographs, this is exactly what happens.

A new instrument—the telescope—had provided Galileo with convincing evidence that Copernicus was right. As others focused their telescopes on Venus and Mercury (which also shows phases), the moons of Jupiter, our own mountainous and scarred moon, and the changing spots on the sun, they too had to acknowledge that we live in a heliocentric solar system whose dimensions dwarf our own tiny planet.

PROJECT 12

From the size of Venus at various phases, you can see that it appears to grow smaller as we see more of it. Given the radii of the orbits of Venus and Earth in Table 1, and recognizing that these orbits are approximate but not perfect circles, does the apparent size of the planet agree reasonably well with its distances from Earth?

The Orbital Radius of an Outer Planet

One way to measure the radius of a planet outside Earth's orbit is shown in Figure 14. The date and time is recorded when Jupiter, Earth, and the sun are in line. A second observation is made when Jupiter and the sun are 90° apart as

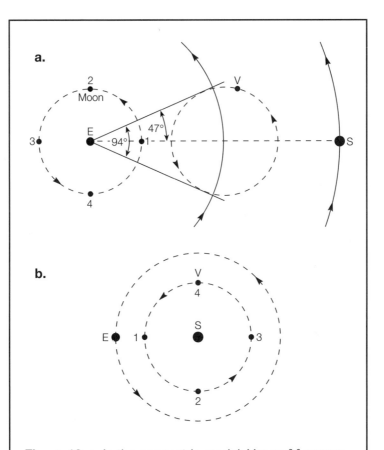

Figure 13 a. In the geocentric model, Venus (V) moves along the circular epicycle (broken line) as it orbits Earth (E) with the sun (S). As you can see, Venus can never appear full in this model because it always lies between Earth and Sun. This model can explain the moon's phases—(1) new; (2) first quarter; (3) full; (4) last quarter—because the moon does orbit Earth.
b. A heliocentric system can explain the phases of Venus. When Earth and Venus are in line on the same side of the sun, Venus is new (1). When Venus and Earth are on opposite sides of sun, Venus is full (3). We see a half Venus when it is at (2) and (4).

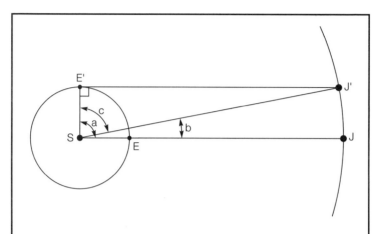

Figure 14 In the drawing, S is the sun, E and E' and J and J' are the positions of Earth and Jupiter separated by an interval of 87.5 days, a = 86.2°, b = 7.28°, and c = a – b = 78.9°.

viewed from Earth. This change in the angular separation of Jupiter and the sun is found to take 87.5 days. Since we know the Earth's period (the time of one revolution) is 365.25 days, angle a can be easily determined:

$$a = (87.5 \text{ days}/365.25 \text{ days}) \times 360° = 86.2°.$$

Jupiter's period is 11.8 years or 4,329 days. Consequently, angle b is 7.3°. As you can see, angle $c = a - b = 86.2° - 7.3° = 78.9°$. By drawing right triangle SE'J' to scale, or by using trigonometry, you can show that SJ', the radius of Jupiter's orbit, is 5.2 times as large as E'S, which is Earth's orbital radius. Consequently, the radius of Jupiter's orbit according to these observations is 5.2 AU.

Later, Jean Dominique Cassini (1625–1712) in Paris and Jean Richer (1630–1696) in French Guiana, about 8,000 kilometers (5,000 mi.) away, simultaneously viewed Mars against the background of the distant stars. By comparing the parallax of Mars against the distant stars from opposite ends of this large base line, Cassini calculated that Mars is about 80 million kilometers from the Earth. Observations similar to those used to measure Jupiter's orbital radius, showed that Mars is 1.53 AU from the sun. Cassini's experiment allowed him to calculate the value of the AU in kilometers:

$$1.53 \text{ AU} - 1.0 \text{ AU} = 80{,}000{,}000 \text{ km} = 8.0 \times 10^7 \text{ km}$$
$$0.53 \text{ AU} = 8.0 \times 10^7 \text{ km}$$
$$8.0 \times 10^7 \text{ km}/0.53 \text{ AU} = X/1.0 \text{ AU}; X = 1.5 \times 10^8 \text{ km}.$$

Once Cassini had established the Earth–sun distance, it was possible to determine the actual radii of all the planets' orbits.

PROJECT 13

Copy Table 1 onto a sheet of paper. Then, using the value of the AU (1.5×10^8 kilometers), add a column to the table to show the actual radii of the all the planets' orbits in kilometers.

At Last! Parallax Among the Stars

As telescopes improved, astronomers learned to measure star positions with great accuracy. Tycho Brahe, who lived before telescopes were invented, had been able to measure the positions of stars and planets to within 2 minutes (2/60 of a degree) of arc, which is the limit for naked-eye astronomy. With telescopes, it became possible to measure angles to seconds (1/60 of a minute or 1/3,600 of a degree) or even to fractions of a second of arc. Using telescopes and the opposite ends of Earth's orbit as a base line, astronomers were able to detect tiny shifts in the positions of stars that are closer than the background—or more distant—stars that still revealed no parallax with respect to one another.

The nearest star, Alpha Centauri, shows 0.75 seconds of

parallax and is about 4r light-years away. Sirius, the brightest star in the sky, has 0.38 seconds of parallax and is nearly 9 light-years from Earth. The parallax found for some of the nearer stars should not be confused with the so-called *proper motions* of stars; that is, their consistent angular motion in a particular direction. (This may amount to several seconds of arc each year.) As you might guess, due to their proximity, the nearer stars generally have the largest proper motion. Consequently, stars must be observed over several years to distinguish parallax from proper motion.

How Can We Be Sure the Earth Is Rotating?

Through the work of Galileo, Kepler, and observations made with telescopes, Copernicus's heliocentric model of the solar system gained increasing acceptance. In addition, the discovery of parallax among the stars was convincing evidence that the Earth moves along an orbit. After Newton developed his laws of motion and gravitational attraction, which explained the motion of celestial as well as earthly bodies, few doubted that the Earth rotates as it revolves in its orbit about the sun. However, because the evidence remained circumstantial, a few people still asked, "What direct proof is there to show that the Earth really does turn? We certainly don't feel any motion or see any evidence of its motion."

In 1851, French physicist Jean Foucault (1819–1868) provided the first direct evidence that the Earth really does turn. He built a 61-meter (200-ft.) long pendulum with a 27-kilogram (60-lb.) *bob* that he suspended from the dome of the Pantheon in Paris. He pulled the bob to one side with a cord, which he tied to a wall. Then, to be certain he gave the bob no motion to either side of a straight-line swing, he burned the string to release the bob. (You may have seen a Foucault pendulum at a science museum.) Sometimes the pendulum bob leaves tracks in the sand as the Earth turns be-

Focault's pendulum, seen in this woodcutting, provided clear evidence that Earth rotates.

neath it; sometimes it knocks over pegs placed beside its back-and-forth path.

Since the only force acting on the pendulum bob was the downward force of gravity, Foucault reasoned that a swinging pendulum should maintain its plane of swing. In other words, there is no force pushing the bob sideways. However, if the Earth rotates, the plane of the pendulum's swing should *appear* to change as the Earth turns beneath it.

Think of the pendulum's rotation as measuring the rate at which the Earth turns about a line connecting the pendulum's point of support with the center of the Earth. The effect is easiest to visualize at the North Pole. Looking down from a point above the Pole to the center of the Earth, we would see the Earth turn 360° beneath the pendulum's back-and-forth path once every 24 hours. However, if you were to look down from a stationary position onto a pendulum swinging above the Earth's equator, you would see the Earth moving west to east, but the Earth would not appear to rotate beneath the pendulum. Between the Pole and the equator, you would see some rotation coupled with some west-to-east motion. The farther south you moved, the slower would be the rate of rotation. Foucault showed that the time for the pendulum to make one complete rotation would be given by

$$T = 24 \text{ hr.}/\sin L,$$

where T is the time to make one rotation and L is the latitude of the pendulum. At 30° latitude, the time to make one rotation would be

$$T = 24 \text{ hr.}/\sin 30° = 24 \text{ hr.}/0.5 = 48 \text{ hr.}$$

PROJECT 14

Using a pocket calculator or a table of sines, answer the following questions. What would be the period (time to make one rotation) of a Foucault pendulum at a latitude of 45°N? What would be its period at the Tropic of Cancer (latitude 23.5°N)? At the Arctic Circle (latitude 66.5°N)? At the Antarctic Circle (latitude 66.5°S)? At the South Pole (90°S)?

The Foucault Pendulum, a Model

You might like to build a Foucault pendulum as a long-term science project, but to understand the principle you can do something considerably easier. You can make a small model of such a pendulum. First, cut a piece of thin cardboard to match the top of an old record-player turntable or a lazy Susan. Then, tie one end of a piece of string to a heavy metal nut or washer. (The string and nut or washer will act as the pendulum bob.) Tape the other end of the string to the top of a small box fixed to the turntable or lazy Susan with tape as shown in Figure 15.

Draw a straight line along the cardboard, under the mo-

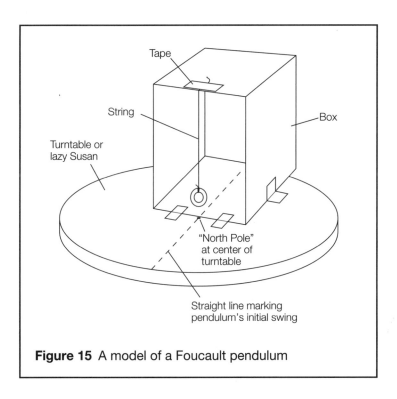

Figure 15 A model of a Foucault pendulum

tionless bob, and into the box. Make a dot directly under the pendulum bob. The dot will represent Earth's North Pole. Pull the bob back a short distance and release it so that it swings back and forth just above the line. Then slowly turn the turntable or lazy Susan. From this model you can see how the plane of swing of a Foucault pendulum, marked by the line you drew and the point of the pendulum's suspension, would appear to rotate.

Next, ignore local gravity for a moment and imagine your model Foucault pendulum tipped 90° and swinging at Earth's equator. (Think of the model as taped to the edge of the turntable or lazy Susan with the bob free to swing up and down.) Perhaps you can see that at the equator the pendulum would not appear to rotate beneath the line you drew.

The pendulum's point of support and, therefore, the string and the bob turn with the Earth. You might think that this would cause the direction of swing to change. To see that the plane of the swing is not affected by turning the point of support, remove the model pendulum you made from the box. Hold the end of the string with your thumb and fingers and set the bob swinging back and forth along a fixed plane. Gently twist the end of the string. Does the bob turn with the string? Does the direction of the bob's swinging path change?

Other Evidence of Earth's Rotation: Coriolis Forces

The apparent rotation of a body moving over the Earth's surface is not limited to Foucault pendulums. A rotating Earth gives rise to fictitious forces known as *Coriolis forces*. Bodies such as long-range projectiles or air masses moving north or south across the Earth's Northern Hemisphere appear to be deflected to the right of their paths as they move—as if a force were pushing them. Since there is no force that can cause such a deflection, the change in direction is said to be due to a fictitious force. But if there is no force, why do they appear to move to the right as they travel?

Imagine a long-range projectile fired northward from the equator. Because it was fired at the equator, it had a velocity of 1,700 kilometers per hour (1,050 mph) eastward as well as its northward velocity. The eastward velocity is due to the rotation of the Earth. Remember, the Earth's equator is 40,000 kilometers (25,000 mi.) in circumference, and it rotates once every 24 hours. Consequently, the velocity of any object resting on the equator is

$$40,000 \text{ km}/24 \text{ hr.} = 1,700 \text{ km/hr.}$$

The velocity of an object resting on the North Pole is zero because the pole, being at the end of the Earth's axis, turns in place. Moving from the equator toward the North Pole, the speed at which the Earth turns eastward gradually decreases. At 45°N latitude, the circumference of the line of latitude is 28,350 kilometers (17,620 mi.). The velocity of the Earth's surface at this latitude is, therefore,

$$28,350 \text{ km}/24 \text{ hr.} = 1,200 \text{ km/hr.}$$

When the above northward-launched projectile reaches a latitude of 45°, the ground beneath it is turning eastward at only 1,200 kilometers per hour (750 mph). To people observing the projectile from 45° latitude, it appears to have an eastward velocity (relative to them) of

$$1,700 \text{ km/hr.} - 12,000 \text{ km/hr.} = 500 \text{ km/hr.}$$

The projectile appears to be curving eastward, or to the right, when viewed from the frame of reference of the projectile.

Similarly, a projectile launched southward from the North Pole will have a westward velocity relative to points to the south because its eastward velocity was zero. Objects at rest on the Earth at 45°N latitude have an eastward velocity of 1,200 kilometers per hour (750 mph). You can easily demonstrate that such a projectile would appear to have a westward velocity by carrying out the following activity.

ACTIVITY 3

The Coriolis Effect

To demonstrate the westward velocity of a projectile launched southward from the North Pole you will need a lazy Susan or an old record turntable, scissors, cardboard, tape, and a pencil. Cut a circular piece of cardboard to match the shape of the lazy Susan or turntable, make a hole at its center to represent the North Pole, and tape it to the device. Switch on the turntable or have someone turn the lazy Susan by hand so that it rotates from west to east as the Earth does. Place the tip of a pencil at the "North Pole" and pull it "southward" (straight toward the edge of the cardboard disk) as the "Earth" turns beneath it.

The moving tip of the pencil represents the projectile moving southward across the Earth's surface. Which way does the line appear to curve as it moves? Why?

Winds accompanying weather patterns that move north or south show the Coriolis effect. Even falling bodies reveal this effect. A lead ball dropped from a tall tower will land slightly east of the point directly beneath it. The ball at the top of the tower has an eastward velocity slightly greater than the ground beneath it because its distance from the center of the Earth is greater than that of the ground directly below it. As it falls, the ball retains that eastward velocity and therefore strikes the ground at a point slightly east of the line connecting the ball and the center of the Earth.

Suppose the tower is 100 meters tall. The eastward velocity of the Earth's surface at the base of the tower is $2\pi r/24$ hr., where r is the distance from the Earth's axis to its surface. The eastward velocity of the ball at the top of the tower is $2\pi(r + 100 \text{ m})/24$ hr.

Show that the eastward velocity of a lead ball at the top of a 100-meter tower at latitude 45° is about 26 meters per hour relative to the ground beneath it. A lead ball dropped from this height will take about 4.5 seconds to reach the ground. How far east of the point directly beneath it will the ball land?

CHAPTER 3

Measuring Distances on Earth

Earth, as you have read, is 150 million kilometers (94 million mi.) from the sun. Pluto, the outermost planet in our solar system, is nearly 6 billion kilometers (3.8 billion mi.) from the sun. Still, even Pluto's radius of orbit is less than 1/1,000 of a light-year, a barely detectable distance along the 100,000 light-year diameter of our Milky Way galaxy. Our entire solar system is but a tiny speck in the immense universe that surrounds us, a universe estimated to have a diameter of 20 to 30 billion light-years.

Given the size of the universe, you would think that finding our position on such a tiny planet would be a simple matter, but if you have ever been lost, you know what it means to wonder where on Earth you are. So let's get down to Earth! Let's face the task of finding our own paths and positions as we move across the Earth's surface, which, to us, seems so vast because, comparatively, we are so small. Each two steps we take (called a *pace*) is approximately equal to our own height, and 1 mile (5,280 feet) was originally a distance equal to 1,000 paces of a marching Roman army. A hike around the world would require 25 million paces—a good 2-year-long walk!

Measuring distances and angles is an essential part of drawing maps of the Earth's surface—diagrams that can help us to know where on Earth we are. When measuring large distances, remember that the seemingly flat surface of the Earth is really part of a large spherical surface. At this sphere's equator, the circumference is very nearly 40,000 kilometers (25,000 mi.). At points midway between the equator and the North Pole (latitude = 45°), the distance around the Earth along a line of latitude is only 28,300 kilometers (18,000 mi.). At the Arctic Circle, the distance around a line parallel to the equator is a mere 16,000 kilometers (10,000 mi.), and, of course, at the North Pole itself, the distance around the Earth is but the turn of a point, a distance of zero.

INVESTIGATION 9

Using Parallax to Measure Distance

Cassini's measurement of the distance to Mars by means of parallax, discussed in the previous chapter, can be used to measure distances on Earth. As you know, parallax, the apparent shift of one object with respect to another when an observer views them from opposite ends of a base line, occurs when the objects are at different distances from a base line. Objects that are the same distance away show no parallax.

To use parallax to measure the distance to an object on Earth, sight on two objects that form a straight line but are located at very different distances from you. One object might be a hill, a house, a monument, a tree, or another easily distinguishable object several hundred meters away. The other, more distant object could be a mountain peak, a steeple, a tall building, or something else far away. The more distant object should be so far away that the light rays from it are very nearly parallel when they reach your eyes. Walk a few steps at right angles to your line of sight and look again. The two objects no longer lie along the same line of sight.

To measure the distance to the nearer object, you can use the more distant object as a reference point. Parallax between the near and the very distant object will allow you to find the distance to the nearer object. You will need a sheet of cardboard like the one shown in Figure 16a, a sheet of paper taped to the cardboard, three common pins, and a measuring tape.

With the nearer and more distant objects in line, use two pins to establish a sightline from your eye through the two pins to the two objects (Position 1 in Figure 16b). Now use the measuring tape to measure out a base line of 30 to 40 meters perpendicular to your line of sight. Move to the other end of the base line (Position 2 in Figure 16b) and again sight along the two pins to the distant reference—the steeple, mountain peak, or whatever. Use the third pin (pin 3) and pin 1 to mark a new line of sight to the nearer object. Because of parallax, the nearer object has now shifted its apparent position relative to the more distant object.

The triangle on the board established by pins 1, 2, and 3 is similar to, but much smaller than, the triangle on the ground (triangle ABC in Figure 16c). By measuring the actual base line on the ground and the smaller distances between pins 1 and 3 and pins 2 and 3 on the cardboard, you can determine the distance to the nearer object. (The dotted sightlines to the distant reference object are essentially parallel because the reference object is so far away.) According to your measurements, what is the distance to the nearer object?

How could you determine the distance to the nearer object if it were not possible to align it with the distant reference object? See Figure 16d.

Carry out this same experiment using a camera instead of the board and pins. You will need to know the focal length of the camera, which constitutes one leg of the small triangle, and the parallax of the nearer object whose distance you are trying

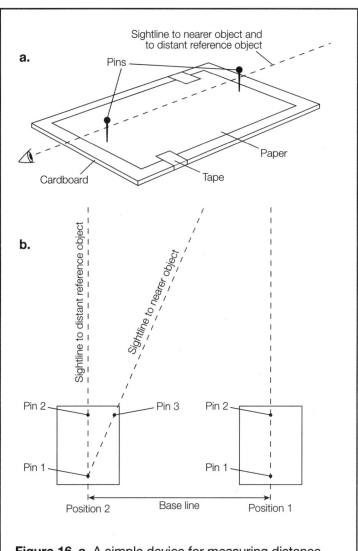

Figure 16 a. A simple device for measuring distance by means of parallax. **b.** Establishing sightlines when the near and distant object are aligned (position 1) at one end of a base line, and when they are not (position 2) at the other end of the base line.

Figure 16 continues on next page

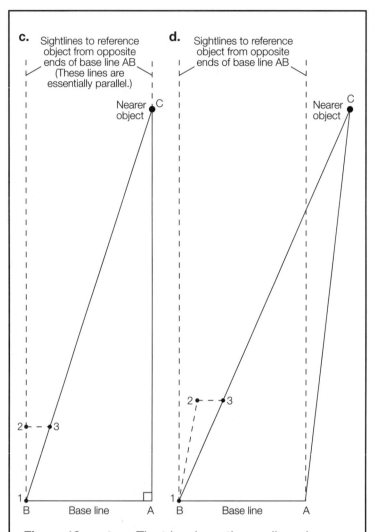

c. Sightlines to reference object from opposite ends of base line AB (These lines are essentially parallel.)

Nearer object C

2 – 3

1
B   Base line   A

d. Sightlines to reference object from opposite ends of base line AB

Nearer object C

2 – 3

1
B   Base line   A

Figure 16 cont. c. The triangle on the cardboard established by pins 1, 2, and 3 is similar to triangle ABC on the ground where AB is the base line. **d.** Even if the nearer and more distant object do not initially lie on the same line of sight, the triangle on the cardboard (123) is similar to the triangle on the ground (ABC).

to determine. Why must the apparent shift of the nearer object be measured on a negative or proof sheet, not on an enlarged print? Why did Cassini have to use a base line of several thousand miles to measure the distance to Mars?

Finding Distance Using Similar Triangles

To estimate the cost involved in building a bridge across a swift-flowing river, an engineer might decide to begin by measuring the river's width. This could be done by establishing a sightline across the river using several sticks (X, Y, and Z in Figure 17) to establish a sightline to an object (O) close to the shore on the other side of the river. Stick X in Figure 17 is at the edge of the river on the near side.

Next, a line YW could be established perpendicular to the

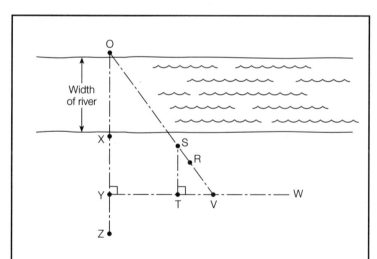

Figure 17 Similar triangles can be used to find the width of a river, lake, canyon, or other distance that might be difficult to measure directly.

sightline. At some point along the perpendicular, a second sightline (ORV) could be made to the object on the other side of the river. At T, a line perpendicular to the line YVW can be constructed and extended until it meets the sightline ORV at S.

Since triangle STV is similar to the larger triangle OYV, we can establish the length of OY because OY/VY = ST/VT. The distance XY can then be measured and subtracted from OY to find the distance from O to X—the width of the river.

Use a similar method to find the width of another river or the distance between two arbitrary points established with sticks or some other markers. What materials will you need?

INVESTIGATION 11

Finding Distance Using a Range Finder

Today, radar is generally used to find the speeds of and distances to cars, planes, ships, and other objects, but you can build a simple range finder that uses a reflected image to measure distances. You will need some wood, paper, tape, glue, a common pin, a thumbtack, and two small mirrors—one fixed and one movable. Each mirror should be about 2 inches long and 1 inch wide.

The base line for this range finder is the distance between the fixed mirror and the movable mirror. These two mirrors are glued to the long sides of the two triangular wooden blocks, as shown in Figure 18. One of the blocks is then glued to a corner of the 4 inch × 24 inch base. (In this figure, the symbol " is used to indicate inches.)

One end of a long, movable marking stick (the thin stick in the base of a window shade works well) is attached to the base with the thumbtack. The stick is free to rotate about the tack. The triangular wooden block that supports the movable mirror is then glued to the fixed end of the movable marking stick.

Before using a range finder to measure distances, you must calibrate it. To do this, sight across the top of the fixed mirror

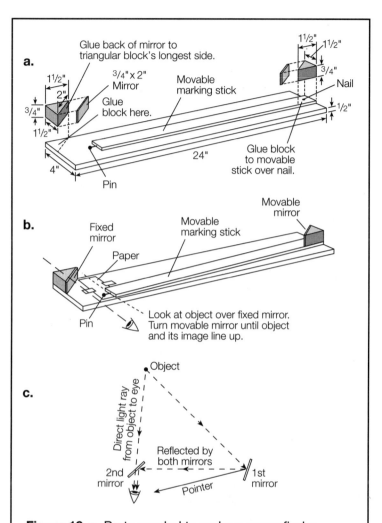

a. Glue back of mirror to triangular block's longest side.

$1^1/_2$"

$^3/_4$" x 2" Mirror

$1^1/_2$"

2"

$^3/_4$"

$1^1/_2$"

4"

Glue block here.

Movable marking stick

Pin

24"

$1^1/_2$" $1^1/_2$"

$^3/_4$"

Nail

$^1/_2$"

Glue block to movable stick over nail.

b. Fixed mirror

Paper

Movable marking stick

Movable mirror

Pin

Look at object over fixed mirror. Turn movable mirror until object and its image line up.

c.

Object

Direct light ray from object to eye

Reflected by both mirrors

2nd mirror

Pointer

1st mirror

Figure 18 a. Parts needed to make a range finder. **b.** The range finder with parts assembled. **c.** Diagram showing how light rays from a distant object reach your eye both directly and by reflection. Changing the distance to the object will change the angle the first mirror must be turned to reflect the object's image to the second mirror.

to some very distant object. Then turn the movable marking stick until the image of the distant object is reflected in the fixed mirror. Carefully move the stick until the image of the distant object (as seen in the fixed mirror) lines up with the distant object itself (as seen over the top of that mirror). Use a pencil to make a mark on the paper just beneath the tip of the pin head. Label this mark infinity (∞).

Next, place a stake vertically into the ground, or find a post, pole, or thin tree trunk. Stand exactly 5 meters from the vertical object and again turn the marking stick on the range finder until the doubly reflected image of the post (as seen in the fixed mirror) lines up with the post itself (as viewed over the top of the same mirror). Make a new mark beneath the pin head and label it "5 m." Repeat the procedure for distances of 10, 15, 20, 25, etc. meters until the lines are too closely spaced to make further calibration feasible.

Use your range finder to measure the distance to a variety of objects that fall within its range. Compare your measurements using the range finder with more direct measurements using a measuring tape. How closely do your measurements agree? Over what distances is the range finder accurate? How could you change the range finder so that it could be used to measure larger distances? Test your hypothesis by building and using such an improved range finder.

INVESTIGATION 12

Measuring Distance with Wheels

You have examined several ways to measure distance. A tape measure is probably the most accurate and useful if you are making maps. A pedometer, which is useful on long hikes, especially in the wilderness, is also reasonably accurate once it has been calibrated. A rocker arm inside the pedometer responds to the impact of each step by descending and springing back, thus moving a ratchet wheel. By walking a previously measured mile with the pedometer on your body, you can make a good estimate of the number of steps you take per mile. Once you've made this calibration, you can use the pedometer to estimate distance. Of course, walking through brush, soft ground, or steep inclines will reduce the accuracy of the pedometer.

You may have seen people pushing a wheel at the end of

This "wheel on a stick" can be used to measure distances.

a stick along a roadway. A wheel can be used to measure distance quite accurately. Each time the wheel makes a turn, it travels a distance equal to its circumference. If its circumference is 3 feet and it makes 100 turns, you know the distance that the wheel has rolled is 300 feet.

You can make a measuring wheel by using your own bicycle. If the front wheel can be easily removed, build a handle that you can attach to the wheel's axle and use it to push the wheel. You could also leave the wheel on the bicycle. In either case, you will need to make a chalk or pen mark on the wheel's circumference. With the mark at the very bottom of the wheel, make a corresponding mark on a sidewalk or pavement. Roll the wheel through several turns and stop with the mark at the bottom of the wheel. Make a second mark on the pavement beside the mark on the wheel. How can you find the distance traveled by the wheel when it makes one turn? What is the circumference of the wheel? Using the information you have obtained, predict the wheel's diameter. Then measure the diameter of the wheel. Was your prediction close to the actual diameter?

INVESTIGATION 13

Measuring Distance by Pacing

You can make very reasonable approximations of distance if you know the length of your pace. A pace (two steps) is the distance between the point where the heel of one foot is raised to the point where the same heel is put down again following a step by the other foot. A normal pace is about 1.5 meters (5 ft.), but an individual's pace depends on the length of his or her legs.

To find the length of your pace, use a measuring tape or a football field to establish a distance of 300 feet. [A football field is 300 feet (100 yards) from goal line to goal line.] Walk the 300 feet as you normally would, counting the paces as you go. How many paces did it take to walk 300 feet? How can you find the length of your pace? How many paces would it take to walk 1 mile? To walk 1 kilometer?

Find the area of a football or soccer field using paces.

On a wilderness hike or trip, it is useful to know how far you travel so that you can follow your progress on a map. To see how you could use your pace to measure distance on a long hike, count out 100 pebbles and put them in your pocket. As you walk, count your paces. Each time you have walked 100 paces, drop a pebble. Then start counting your paces again. How many pebbles will you have dropped after walking 1 mile? After walking 1 kilometer? When all the pebbles are gone, how far will you have walked?

INVESTIGATION 14

Distance from Dead Reckoning

If you walk at a reasonably constant speed, the approximate distance you travel can be found by what is called *dead reckoning*, the product of velocity and time. For example, if you walk due north at a speed of 4 kilometers per hour (2.5 mph) for 3 hours, the distance you travel northward will be about 12 kilometers (4 km/hr. $\times$ 3 hr. = 12 km). We say "about 12 kilometers" because your walking speed is not exactly constant and depends on the terrain over which you move.

To see how accurately you can measure distance using dead reckoning, you will first need to measure your walking speed. You can do this by walking across a football field or some comparable distance (300 feet) at your normal pace. At the moment you start your walk, start a stopwatch or note the exact time on a watch with a second hand. When you reach the end of the known distance, stop the stopwatch or note the time to the nearest second on a watch.

Use the distance walked and the elapsed time to calculate your walking speed. How fast do you walk in feet per second? In miles per hour? In kilometers per hour? (Remember, there are 1.6 kilometers in a mile, 5,280 feet in a mile, 1,000 meters in a kilometer, and 3,600 seconds in an hour.)

After recording the exact time, start walking from some well-established point. Walk at your normal pace for at least an hour. Note the exact position where you stop and the exact time. Use dead reckoning to calculate how far you walked. To check your estimate, use the odometer on an automobile, the measuring wheel you used in Investigation 12, or the number of paces you walked. How does the distance you calculated using dead reckoning compare with the distance you measured?

Carry out a similar experiment in a car. Record the odometer reading when you start. Then ask the driver to drive, as much as possible, at several different constant legal speeds while you record the time traveled at each speed. At the end of the trip, calculate the distance traveled using dead reckoning. How does the calculated distance compare with the difference in odometer readings?

In the past, sailing ships measured the distance they traveled by dead reckoning. A sailor would throw a block of wood attached to a knotted line overboard. Once it hit the water, the block would remain in place as more and more line was released. The knots had been tied in the line at known separations so that the sailor, by counting the knots, could tell how much line had been released. While one sailor was releasing the knotted line, another would turn over an hourglass to measure time. From the length of line and the time, it was easy to calculate the ship's speed, usually in knots (1 knot = 1 nautical mile per hour). Once its speed was known, the distance traveled along a set course could be determined by dead reckoning. Of course, changes in wind speed or direction would require new measurements of speed.

At best, dead reckoning gave only an approximate position of the ship. Due to inaccuracies in the measurements and the effects of ocean currents, a sea captain might discover that he was several hundred miles east or west of where he thought he was.

INVESTIGATION **15**

Shortest Routes Along the Earth

You may have wondered why an airplane flying from New York to Tokyo travels across the Arctic rather than following a line of latitude slightly south of 40°N. You can discover the reason quite easily by using a string and a globe. To calibrate the string, place it around the globe's equator. Lay the string on a ruler or yardstick to determine the length of string needed to reach around the globe's equator. The distance around the real Earth's equator is 40,000 kilometers (24,900 mi.). If the distance around your globe is 38 inches, then each inch on the globe corresponds to 655 miles (24,900 mi./38 in. = 655 mi./in.).

Now use the same string to find the shortest distance from New York to Tokyo. You can do this by laying the string on the globe. What is the shortest path along the globe from New York to Tokyo?

What is the shortest route from Los Angeles to New Delhi, India? From Chicago to Moscow, Russia? From New Orleans to Hong Kong?

Great Circle Routes

The previous investigation revealed that the shortest routes between points on Earth are usually not along lines of latitude. If you measure shortest routes carefully, you will find that they lie along what are called great circles. As you learned in Chapter 1, a great circle is a circle on the surface of a sphere whose center lies at the center of the sphere. Such a circle divides the globe into two equal hemispheres. The arc of a great circle is always the shortest distance between two points on a sphere. On Earth, all lines of longitude are great circles. Which line of latitude is a great circle?

It is usually easy for airplanes to follow great-circle routes. Oceangoing ships, however, often have to deviate from great circle routes because of land barriers, icebergs, or unfavorable ocean currents.

CHAPTER 4

Magnets, Compasses, and Directions

In Chapter 3 you found ways to measure distance, but distance alone will not help you find your way on the Earth's surface. You also need to know in which direction you should travel. For centuries people have relied on compasses for direction. A compass is a small magnet that is free to turn in a magnetic field. The Earth's magnetic field controls a compass.

INVESTIGATION 16

Magnets and Magnetic Fields

Tape a sheet of white paper to a thin sheet of cardboard and place the cardboard on a bar magnet. Sprinkle some iron filings onto the paper.

If you don't have iron filings, you can make some from a new pad of fine steel wool. Find the end of the roll and unroll it a few centimeters. Trim the end and sides of the roll with scissors to eliminate long stray fibers. Then cut very narrow strips from the roll. Make the strips as narrow as you can so that the fibers will be very short. Let the tiny pieces of steel fall onto a sheet of paper. You can then use the sheet as a chute to empty the particles into an old salt shaker.

Sprinkle the filings on the paper you placed on the bar magnet. Tapping the paper allows the iron particles to move freely. Describe the pattern you see.

Magnets, Compasses, and Magnetic Fields

The pattern you saw in the previous investigation is the result of a magnetic field that surrounds the magnet. The field around the magnet is somewhat like the *gravitational field* that surrounds the Earth. The gravitational field is caused by the force (gravity) that the Earth's matter (mass) exerts on every other mass, including you and me. The Earth's gravitational field can be represented by lines that point toward the Earth's center (Figure 19). The direction of these lines is given by the direction in which the force acts. Objects fall toward the center of the Earth because that is the direction in which gravity pulls them. Where the lines are close together, near the Earth's surface, the force is strong. As the lines grow farther apart with increasing distance from the Earth, the force becomes weaker.

The field surrounding a bar magnet is caused by a magnetic force, but unlike gravity, which always attracts (pulls masses together), magnetic forces repel as well as attract. As you probably know, a bar magnet has two poles, a south pole and a north pole. Opposite poles of two bar magnets (north and south) attract one another, but like poles (north and north or south and south) repel each other.

In the late 1200s, Marco Polo returned to Venice from China, bringing with him a compass, an instrument that had been used in the Orient for centuries but was unknown in

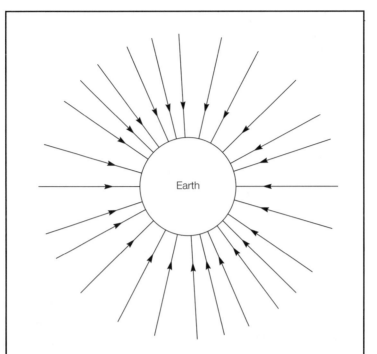

Figure 19 Earth's gravitational field, the force it exerts per kilogram, can be represented by lines. The arrowheads give the direction of the field. The number of lines per area represents the strength of the field.

Europe. In the 1500s, English scientist William Gilbert (1544–1603) demonstrated that compasses are really small magnets. Compass needles attract or repel each other in the same way as magnets. If a bar magnet is suspended from a thread, it orients itself in a north–south direction, just as a compass needle does. Gilbert defined the end of the compass needle or magnet that was northernmost when motion ceased—the end that "points" north—as the north or north-seeking pole.

It was Gilbert who first suggested that the Earth is like a giant magnet. Its field encompasses the entire Earth and resembles the field of a huge bar magnet (Figure 20). Since opposite magnetic poles attract and Gilbert defined the north-seeking pole of a magnet or compass needle as the end that was northernmost, it follows that the Earth's magnetic pole, which is located in northern Canada and is moving slowly northwestward, must be a south-seeking magnetic pole. Similarly, the Earth's other magnetic pole, which is located near the coast of Antarctica, is a north-seeking magnetic pole. The Earth's magnetic poles, as their longitudes and latitudes indicate, are located more than 1,600 km (1,000 mi.) from the geographic poles.

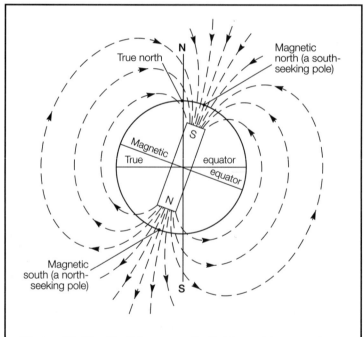

Figure 20 The Earth's magnetic field would suggest that there is a giant bar magnet inside our planet.

When you sprinkle iron filings over a bar magnet, each iron filing acts like a small compass needle. The material inside the bar magnet exerts a force on any magnetic material around it. The direction of the force can be seen by the orientation of the tiny compass needles (iron filings), which together reveal the shape of the field around the magnet. Like gravitational fields, the intensity of the magnetic field is shown by the concentration of the lines.

A compass needle does not point in the same direction everywhere on Earth. If you live in Boston, a compass needle points about 16° west of true north (the direction to the North Pole). In central Texas, it points about 8° east of true north. Along a line from the Florida Panhandle to the western end of Lake Superior, it points very nearly toward true north. The difference in angle between the compass reading and true north is known as the *magnetic declination*. A line of positions along which compass needles point toward true north (declination = 0°) is called an *agonic line*. A line of positions along which compass needles have equal declinations is called an *isogonic line*. Isogonic lines reveal the declination and whether it is east or west of true north. Bear in mind that a compass located on an isogonic line does not point along the isogonic line but in a direction east or west of true north as indicated on the line.

Magnetic declination changes with time and place. William Gilbert's compass pointed 11° east of true north in London. By 1657, a compass in London pointed to true north. Today it points about 7° west of north. At times, the magnetic declination in London has been as much as 25° west of north. Detailed maps of an area will usually include the declination as well as the rate at which it is changing over time.

When Columbus crossed the Atlantic, he noticed that the compass slowly changed its direction with respect to the stars. He kept this a secret from his crew for fear of panic and mutiny.

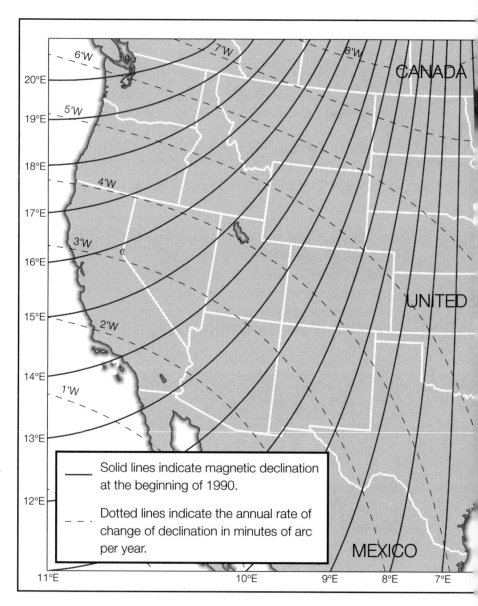

This map of the contiguous United States shows isogonic magnetic declinations as solid lines. The 0° line that extends northward from the Florida Panhandle to the western end of

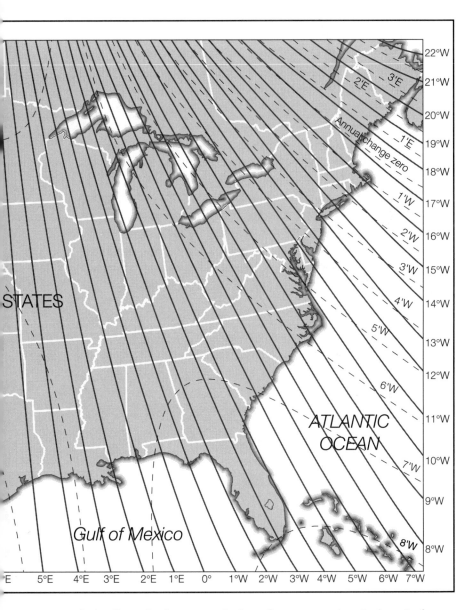

Lake Superior is an agonic line. Compasses located east of the agonic line have westward declinations, while compasses to the west of the line have eastward declinations.

Finding Magnetic Declination Where You Live

To find the magnetic declination at your home, you will need the north–south line you established in Investigation 5. Be sure there are no metallic objects that might be magnetic near that line. Such objects might cause the compass needle to deviate from the direction in which it would normally point. You can see the effect such an object might have by bringing a nail close to the compass. What happens?

Once you are sure there are no magnetic objects near the north–south line you made earlier, hold the compass so that its north–south line (0°–180°) is parallel to your geographic north–south line. What is the orientation of the compass needle? If it lies on the north–south line, which is unlikely, you must live on an isogonic line. If it points west of the north–south line,

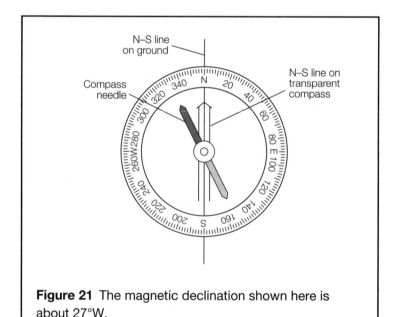

Figure 21 The magnetic declination shown here is about 27°W.

it has a westward declination; if it points east of the north–south line, it has a declination to the east. (See Figure 21.)

If you have an *orienteering compass*, it may have a scale that allows you to read declination once you have set the orienting arrow on true north. What is the declination you find on the compass in degrees east or west of true north? How does your measurement of declination compare with that found on a topographic map of your region?

INVESTIGATION 18

Electricity and Magnetism

Use a lump of clay to support a magnetic compass directly above a long insulated wire, as shown in Figure 22. The wire should be parallel to the compass needle. What happens when you connect the ends of the long wire to a dry-cell or flashlight

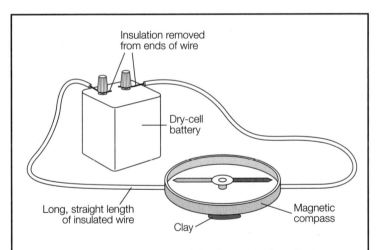

Figure 22 When the ends of the long insulated wire are connected to opposite poles of the battery, a current flows in the wire. What happens to the compass needle?

battery so that an electric current flows inside the wire? What is different if you place the compass underneath the wire?

The effect that you observed in the previous investigation reveals that a magnetic field surrounds an electric current—a flow of electrons within the wire. The Earth's magnetic field is believed to be the result of moving electrical charges deep beneath the Earth's surface. The magnetic field in an ordinary bar magnet is caused by the motion of electrons within the atoms that make up the magnet. These atoms are oriented so that their electrons follow parallel paths and their individual magnetic fields reinforce one another. If a magnet is dropped, it will often lose much of its magnetism because the atoms are jarred out of alignment. The atoms can be "coaxed" back into a pattern that produces a strong magnetic field by placing the weakened magnet in a current carrying *solenoid* (coil of wire with a hollow core) or by stroking it with a strong magnet.

INVESTIGATION 19

Making a Magnet and a Compass

Hold a straight pin or a needle near a compass. It should have no effect on the compass needle. Now stroke the pin or needle with a magnet several times as shown in Figure 23. Always stroke in the same direction. After stroking, bring one end of the pin or needle near one pole of the compass. What happens? How can you determine which end of your pin or needle is the north-seeking pole?

Use a dining fork, a paper clip, or two pieces of grass to gently place your homemade magnet on the surface of water that is free of any soap or detergent. The water's surface tension will support the small strip of metal. Which way does the north-seeking pole of your magnet point when it comes to rest?

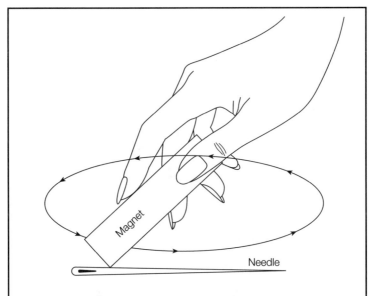

Figure 23 You can make a compass needle by stroking a pin or needle with a magnet.

Could you use such a compass to determine direction in the wilderness?

The Orienteering Compass

Although any compass can be used, an orienteering compass makes finding your way through unfamiliar territory much easier. You can buy an orienteering compass at a store that sells camping or sporting goods for less than $10. As shown in Figure 24, an orienteering compass has a magnetized needle surrounded by a transparent housing that can be rotated on a transparent base plate etched with map scales and directional arrows. The rim of the housing is di-

An orienteering compass makes it easy to find the correct direction of travel.

vided into degrees. The cardinal points, North (N or 0°), East (E or 90°), South (S or 180°), and West (W or 270°), are also indicated on the rim. On the transparent bottom of the housing an orienting arrow always points to North on the dial. When the north-seeking pole of the compass needle, which is usually red, lies directly over the orienting arrow, the compass is oriented so that N (0° or 360°) is directed toward magnetic north.

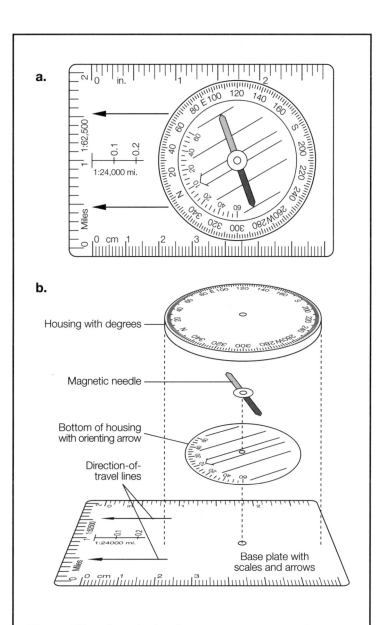

Figure 24 a. An orienteering compass as seen from above **b.** A dissected orienteering compass

Labels in figure:
- Housing with degrees
- Magnetic needle
- Bottom of housing with orienting arrow
- Direction-of-travel lines
- Base plate with scales and arrows

The rectangular base plate has one or more direction-of-travel lines etched on it. If there is more than one, the center line will touch and extend onto the degree-indicating dial edge on the compass housing. The direction-of-travel line indicates the bearing to which the compass has been set. The side edges of the base plate and all direction-of-travel arrows on the base plate are parallel.

INVESTIGATION 20

Finding Directions (Bearings) with an Orienteering Compass

Take an orienteering compass to a hill from which you can view a number of easily identified objects (landmarks). Face the object whose direction (bearing) you wish to determine. Hold the compass in front of you and well away from any magnetic metal, such as a belt buckle, that might affect it. The direction-of-travel arrow(s) should point away from you and straight at the landmark whose bearing you wish to find; that is, it should lie along the same line as the imaginary line connecting your sighting eye with the landmark.

Next, orient the compass by turning the housing until the orienting arrowhead etched on the bottom of the housing lies under the north-seeking pole of the compass needle. (This orienting arrow always points to N on the housing.) Both arrowheads are now at North (0° or 360°) on the compass.

Read the angle (number of degrees) on the far side of the compass indicated by the line of travel. That angle is your direction of travel (bearing) relative to magnetic north. How could you find the bearing relative to true north?

In a similar manner, find the bearings of the other landmarks relative to magnetic north and to true north. Determining a bearing relative to true north is important if you are finding your way with a map as well as a compass.

Using a Compass to Follow a Direction (Bearing)

Pick out a distant landmark and establish its bearing as you did in Investigation 20. In this activity, where a map is not involved, you can use the bearing relative to magnetic north. Suppose the bearing is 90°. This means you need to walk due east to reach the landmark. Whatever the bearing, it is now fixed on your compass unless you change the setting. However, just in case the compass is inadvertently changed, record the bearing so that you will not forget it as you walk toward the distant landmark. You will have no problem walking due east, or whatever the bearing may be, as long as the landmark is visible. However, when the landmark disappears because it is hidden by trees or hills, you must use your compass bearing to determine your direction.

To walk in the correct direction, turn the compass, as before, so that the north-seeking pole of the compass needle lies over the orienting arrow and both point to north (0° or 360°). Sight across the compass to the line-of-travel arrow(s) and walk in the direction it (they) point. If they point at an identifiable landmark (a tree, stump, or other object), walk to this intermediate position. Perhaps from there you will be able to see your original landmark. If not, sight along the same bearing to a new intermediate landmark and walk to it. Continue this process until you reach your original landmark.

Using a Compass to Return to "Camp"

Consider the position from which you started your walk to the distant landmark as "camp." Having reached your destination (the distant landmark), you decide to return to camp. If you traveled due east (90°) from camp to reach your destination, you will have to travel due west (270°) to return to camp. Whatever the direction of your outward journey, you will have to travel in the opposite direction on your return. Thus, the bearing on your return hike (the *back bearing*) will be at an angle of 180° from your initial bearing. If you followed a bearing of 150° to reach your destination, you will have to follow a bearing of 330° to return to camp. If your outward bearing was 240°, you will have to follow a back bearing of 60° to return to camp.

If you have not changed the orienteering compass, all you have to do, after you orient the compass so that the orienting arrow lies under the north-seeking pole of the compass needle, is to hold the compass so that the line-of-travel arrow(s) point toward you rather than away from you. You will be headed toward camp. Just walk in the direction given by the tail(s) of the line-of-travel arrows. If possible, find a landmark along that back bearing or slightly to one side of it. Then walk to that intermediate position. Use the compass, as before, to sight along the same line-of-travel arrow tail(s) to a new intermediate landmark (a tree, stump, or other object) and walk to it. Continue this process until you reach camp.

ACTIVITY 6

Using the Orienteering Compass to Walk a Triangle

An equilateral triangle has three equal sides and three equal angles, all of which must be 60° since a triangle has 180°. (See Figure 25.) If you were to walk along the sides of a large equilateral triangle, you would have to twice change your direction of travel by 120° after traveling equal distances. Walking a third equal distance would then bring you back to your starting point.

Use your orienteering compass to walk the sides of such a triangle. Mark a starting point with an identifiable object such as a washer, a coin, the lid of a can, a golf tee, etc. Face a landmark, orient your compass, and follow the line-of-travel 25

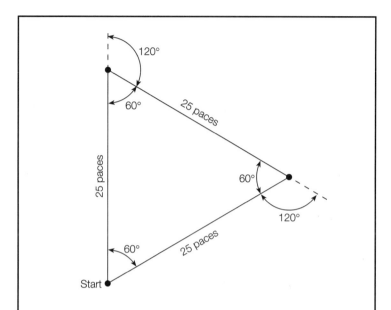

Figure 25 To walk an equilateral triangle, walk 25 paces along a fixed bearing. Stop. Change your direction (bearing) by 120° to your right. Walk another 25 paces. Stop. Change your bearing by another 120° to your right. Walk another 25 paces and you will be back at your starting point.

paces (50 steps) toward the landmark. Stop. Change your bearing by 120° to the right of your original direction of travel and orient your compass again. Turn so that you are ready to walk in the direction indicated by the direction-of-travel line on the compass. Walk 25 paces along this bearing. Stop, and again change your direction of travel by 120° to your right. Walk 25 paces in the direction given by your compass and you should find yourself back at the marker you used to indicate your starting position.

Using your orienteering compass, walk along the perimeter of a square that is 30 paces on a side. Next, walk the perimeter of a hexagon whose sides are each 20 paces long.

PROJECT 16

Walk a right triangle. Make the first side 25 paces long. Turn 90° and walk another 25 paces. Through what angle should you turn before you walk along the triangle's hypotenuse? How many paces can you expect to walk before reaching your starting position?

Walk 30 paces along a straight line. Turn 90°. Then walk 40 paces. Through what angle should you turn so that your next walk of 50 paces brings you back to your starting position? You have walked the perimeter of what kind of figure?

ACTIVITY 7

Hiking Out and Back with an Orienteering Compass

Select a starting point in a large park or in nearby countryside. While it probably isn't necessary for such a short hike, it would be good practice to bracket a base line to either side of your departure point before you set out. Because it is difficult to return to the exact point from which you started, it is good practice to use markers, such as red ribbons, so that you can identify a base line along which your departure and return point lie. Near each marker draw an arrow to indicate the proper direction to your starting point. A lake, river, or road makes a good base line. Once you reach the base line upon your return, you can look for a marker and the nearby pointer, which will direct you to your starting point along the base line.

Start your hike by choosing a fixed direction that you will follow for a 30-minute hike. Orient your compass and determine the bearing of the path you select. If possible, choose a landmark that lies along that bearing and walk to it. Continue along the same direction for the 30-minute hike.

Again, just for practice, record direction and distance as you travel, as well as useful landmarks. Turn and look at these landmarks as you will on your return trip. The same landmark may look quite different against a different background.

You may encounter one or more obstacles along your path. For example, you might encounter a swamp, a pond, or a steep cliff. If you can see around or across the obstacle to a landmark that lies along the bearing you have been following, mark your position in some way and walk around the obstacle to the landmark you identified. Once you reach the landmark, check the back bearing to the position you marked on the other side to be sure it is 180° from the bearing you have been following. With an orienteering compass, all you need to do is see that the direction of travel arrow(s) points toward you as you face the marked position with the oriented compass in your hand.

The simplest way to deal with obstacles that you cannot see around is to follow three sides of a rectangular path around the obstacle. (See Figure 26.) You begin by making a 90° turn. Such a turn is easy to make with an orienteering compass. Suppose you want to turn right. Orient the compass and hold the base plate crosswise in your hand so that you walk perpendicular to the direction indicated by the direction-of-travel arrow, which will now point to your left as you move.

Count your paces as you walk along this bearing 90° to the right of your original path. When you are beyond the obstacle, make another 90° turn so that you are back on your original bearing. Walk in this direction until you are past the obstacle. Then turn another 90°, walk the same number of paces as before, and make one final 90° turn. This should put you back on

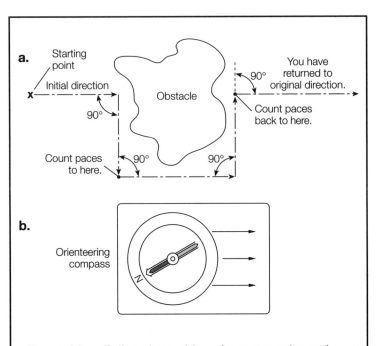

Figure 26 a. Follow three sides of a rectangular path around an obstacle. It will bring you back to your initial path. **b.** In all parts of the rectangular walk, the compass remains oriented as shown.

the same straight-line path you were following before you encountered the obstacle.

After you have walked for 30 minutes, stop. Take a back bearing of 180° from the direction you have been walking and follow it back to "camp." You should be back at your starting point in about 30 minutes unless the first half of your hike has been downhill or uphill.

Somewhere along your hike, you may see a place to which you would like to return for a picnic. To mark your current position so that you can return to it on a later hike, you make two cross bearings by choosing two landmarks that are as close to 90° apart as possible. You turn the direction-of-travel arrow toward one, orient the compass, and record the nature of the landmark and its direction. You then repeat the procedure for the other landmark. The intersection of your bearings will mark a position from which you can see the picnic setting you discovered.

CHAPTER 5

Maps and Mapping

Maps are essentially models of the surface geography of a region. That region may be the entire Earth, an ocean, a country, a state, a county, or someone's property. To people hiking or canoeing through wilderness, a map is their most essential piece of equipment. But the most commonly used maps are road maps, which are two-dimensional, scaled models of the relative locations of roads and towns as seen from above.

All modern maps provide a simplified view of geographic features as seen from above. Since aerial photography became possible, photographs taken from airplanes have served as the basis for maps. These photographs are projected onto a screen and matched with points on the ground whose latitude and longitude are known with great accuracy. The images are then adjusted to fit the known positions on the ground. From these images, maps are drawn and symbols added.

Topographic Maps

While road maps often indicate the height of mountains, they generally omit information about changing elevations that reveal the slope of the land. It is possible, however, to precisely model such features on a flat map. Such maps, known as *topographic maps*, are useful whenever details of an area's terrain need to be known. These maps identify lakes, ponds, streams, roads, trails, quarries, railroad tracks, buildings, bridges, and so on. You can purchase a complete list of symbols or find them in a book on maps, canoeing, or camping.

Topographic maps are scaled so that it is easy to determine the distance between landmarks. Commonly used scales are 1:24,000, 1:50,000, 1:62,500, and 1:250,000. A scale of 1:24,000, for example, means that 1 inch on the map is equivalent to 24,000 inches (2,000 ft.) along the Earth's horizontal surface. (See the Appendix for information about where to buy maps.)

PROJECT 17

Show that a scale of 1:250,000 means that 1 inch on the map is very nearly equivalent to 4 miles and 1 centimeter is equivalent to 2.5 kilometers. Approximately how many feet and miles are represented by 1 inch on maps where the scale factor is 1:25,000? 1:50,000? 1:62,500? Approximately how many meters and kilometers are represented by 1 centimeter on maps with the same scales?

The latitudes covered by a topographic map are indicated along the vertical sides of the map; the longitudes covered by the same map are found along its horizontal (top and bottom) borders. By connecting the corresponding

marks that represent degrees of longitude at the top and bottom of the map, you are drawing meridian lines. These lines, which may or may not be parallel to grid lines on the map, are true north–south lines. If extended far enough, they would reach the Earth's North and South Poles. Horizontal lines connecting the corresponding degrees of latitude at the right and left sides of the map would be lines of latitude parallel to the equator.

Normally, you can expect the top of the map to be north and the bottom to be south. This means that west on the map will be to your left and east to your right. Somewhere on the map you will find an arrow that indicates true north, another arrow that indicates magnetic north, and the angle between them, which gives the declination. But remember, declination may change with time. To know the area's present declination you need to know the date the map was drawn and the rate at which declination is changing. You should be able to find this information on the map.

The thin brown lines on topographic maps are contour lines. They indicate the altitude of the land. The altitude along any single contour line is the same, and a contour interval indicating the difference in altitude between one contour line and the next is usually given on the map. If not, it can be determined. Simply count the number of contour lines between the two contour lines where the elevation is indicated. Find the difference between the two elevations and divide by the number of contour lines that separate them. Military strategists, mountain climbers, highway en-

The photograph (above) shows a portion of Yosemite Valley, California. If you look closely at the topographic map (below), you will see that it represents the same area.

99

gineers, architects, landscapers, hikers, and canoeists are among the people who find such maps useful.

Mapping a Model Terrain

To understand how contour lines are placed on a map, you can start by building a model terrain. Line a large, sturdy cardboard or wooden box with a sheet of clear plastic. Use modeling clay to build a single mountain near the center of the box. Then pour water (1 centimeter deep) into the box. Use a pin or sharp pencil to trace the water line around your clay mountain. The line you have drawn is a contour line. Every point along this line represents the same elevation. In this model, the contour line represents an elevation of 1 centimeter above the bottom of the box, which might represent sea level. A photograph of this clay model taken from above would enable you to identify every point where the elevation was 1 centimeter by looking at the contour line.

Add another 1 centimeter of water to the box and mark a second (2-centimeter) contour line along your clay mountain. Continue adding water in increasing depths of 1 centimeter and marking the corresponding contour lines. When you have finished, you will have a complete series of contour lines, each representing a 1-centimeter increase in elevation.

Now that you have marked the contour lines on the model, you are ready to make a contour map of the model terrain. You do so by transferring these contour lines to a flat sheet of paper and labeling them with the appropriate elevations in centimeters. One way to do this is to photograph the clay model from above, but you can draw a reasonable map by letting your eyes serve as the camera.

Next, make a more complicated model that includes two or three mountains of different heights. Try to vary the slopes on different sides of the mountains to provide an interesting and realistic model of a terrain.

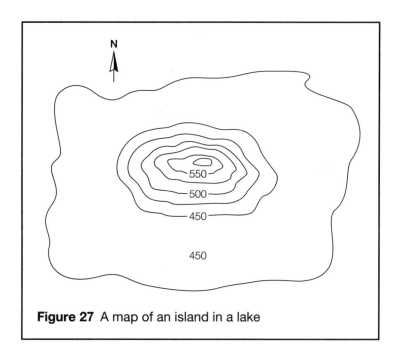

Figure 27 A map of an island in a lake

Repeat the procedure you followed before and prepare a contour map of the model terrain. Compare your contour map with the clay model. What features on the map indicate steep slopes? Shallow slopes? Mountain peaks? Valleys?

Using pencil, paper, and rulers, draw a contour map of an ice cream cone. Then draw a contour map of a hemisphere. If possible, draw a contour map of a pyramid. How do the contour lines reveal the differences among a cone, a hemisphere, and a pyramid?

How could you construct a model terrain from the map shown in Figure 27? One approach would be to trace the closed loops formed by the contour lines onto separate pieces of cardboard. Then cut out each loop and stack them in their proper order with scaled spacers in between. If you wish, you could cover the resulting structure with a thin layer of papier-mâché.

Mapping Hills

To see how real contour maps are made, you will need a tape measure, a plane table, some marking sticks or pegs, and a range rod. You can make a plane table from 15 in. × 15 in. × 0.5 in. piece of plywood together with a 4 ft. × 1 in. × 1 in. stick, four right-angle metal braces, screws, two screw eyes, a small carpenter's level or suitable substitute, and a range rod as shown in Figure 28.

Find a hill or incline that rises from a reasonably level surface. Assign the level an arbitrary altitude of zero unless you happen to know the actual altitude above sea level. Place the plane table at the base of the incline and use a small stick or peg to mark the position of the base of the plane table. Have a partner move the range rod up the incline in front of you until its base is 1 foot above the level ground on which you stand. You can determine this by sighting through the two screw eyes on one side of the plane table. A level (see Figure 28) taped to the table will help you determine when the table is level.

When your line of sight through the screw eyes is in line with the 3-foot line on the range rod, you will know that the elevation of the ground has increased by 1 foot (See Figure 29 on page 104). Mark that elevation in some identifying manner. You might, for example, use blue golf tees to mark one-foot elevations and other colors to mark higher elevations. Then have your partner move the range rod slowly up the incline along the same straight line. When your line of sight through the screw eyes is in line with the 2-foot line on the range rod, you will know that the altitude of the ground has increased by 2 feet. You can mark this and each 1-foot increase in elevation until you reach the top of the incline. Of course, it may be necessary to move your plane table along the hill once your sightline is below the bottom of the range rod.

Repeat the process along other straight lines parallel to the first one and about 10 feet to the right or left. Once you have

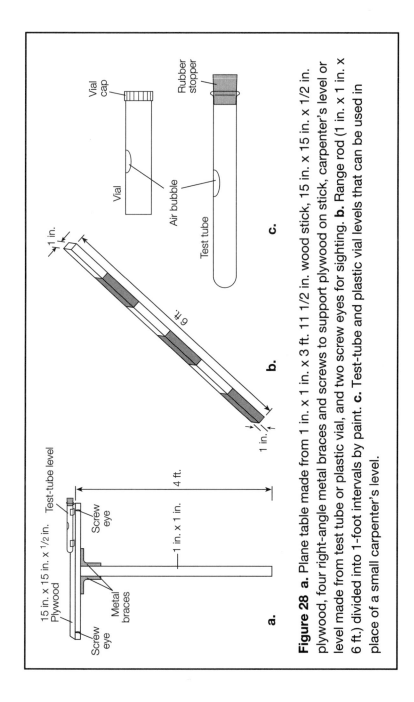

Figure 28 a. Plane table made from 1 in. x 1 in. x 3 ft. 11 1/2 in. wood stick, 15 in. x 15 in. x 1/2 in. plywood, four right-angle metal braces and screws to support plywood on stick, carpenter's level or level made from test tube or plastic vial, and two screw eyes for sighting. **b.** Range rod (1 in. x 1 in. x 6 ft.) divided into 1-foot intervals by paint. **c.** Test-tube and plastic vial levels that can be used in place of a small carpenter's level.

103

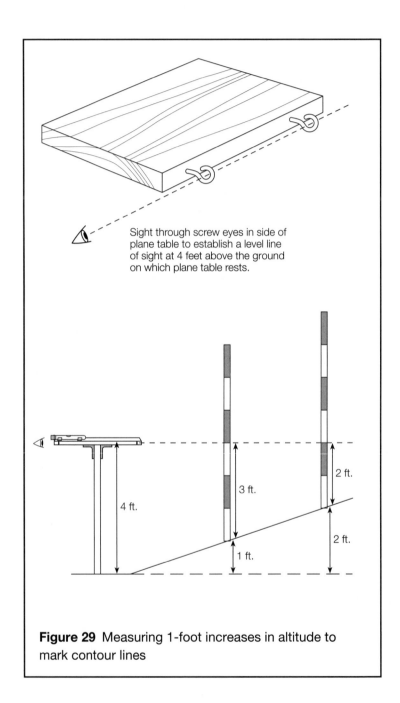

Sight through screw eyes in side of plane table to establish a level line of sight at 4 feet above the ground on which plane table rests.

4 ft.

3 ft.

1 ft.

2 ft.

2 ft.

Figure 29 Measuring 1-foot increases in altitude to mark contour lines

Table 2: Hypothetical Data for Measuring Elevations from the Base of a Hill

Altitude (ft.)	Distances (in feet) from straight base line at the foot of the hill for line number				
	1	2	3	4	5
1	2.0	1.5	2.0	2.5	3.0
2	3.0	3.0	2.5	3.0	3.5
3	3.5	4.0	3.5	3.5	4.0
4	4.0	4.5	4.0	5.0	4.5
5	5.5	6.0	5.0	6.0	5.5
6	6.5	6.5	6.0	7.0	6.5
7	7.0	7.5	6.5	7.5	7.0
8	8.5	8.0	7.5	9.0	9.0

marked the points needed to make contour lines, you can begin recording the horizontal distances between the 1-foot increases in elevation. Use these data to draw a map with contour lines for the hill you measured. Then draw a side view of the hill along one straight line.

Data for a rather steep hill are shown in Table 2. A map of the contour lines based on the data in that table is shown in Figure 30a; a longitudinal view of the hill is shown in Figure 30b. How do these maps compare with yours? How can you use a compass to add a north-pointing arrow to your map?

How could you use the plane table, measuring tape, and range rod to measure and construct contour maps of the altitudes of points at elevations lower than the plane table?

PROJECT 18

A contour map of a hill located on an island in a lake is shown in Figure 27. The elevation of the lake, printed on the

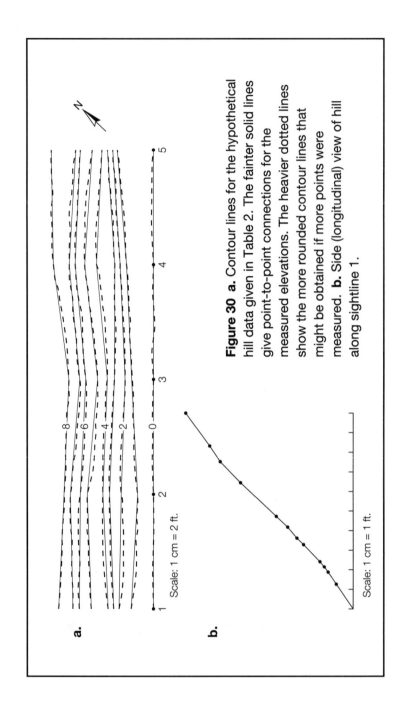

Figure 30 a. Contour lines for the hypothetical hill data given in Table 2. The fainter solid lines give point-to-point connections for the measured elevations. The heavier dotted lines show the more rounded contour lines that might be obtained if more points were measured. **b.** Side (longitudinal) view of hill along sightline 1.

"water," is, of course, constant. What is the approximate length and width of the island? Of the lake? What is the elevation at the top of the hill relative to sea level? What is its altitude relative to the lake? Sketch a scaled side view of the north side of the hill to show its steepness.

Mapping the World

Maps of towns, cities, and even counties were available in the 1400s, but accurate maps of countries and the world were not made until the end of the 1600s. During the late 1600s, Giovanni Domenico Cassini and his staff, with the support of King Louis XIV, prepared the first accurate map of France and of the world at the Paris Observatory.

Cassini, who had measured the distance to Mars and established the value of the astronomical unit (AU), was able to develop a means of calculating time precisely from any place on Earth. He recognized Galileo's discovery of a clock in the sky—the moons of Jupiter—and capitalized on it. Using a telescope to observe the four moons that orbit Jupiter, Cassini determined their periods and could predict the exact time when each would be eclipsed, reach their maximum distance from Jupiter, or emerge from behind the planet. From his observations he was able to write tables that predicted when various events regarding the moons of Jupiter would take place. Since Jupiter is so far away (590 to 960 million kilometers or 370 to 600 million miles), its moons appear the same regardless of your position on Earth. Consequently, an astronomer anywhere in the world could, by using Cassini's tables, determine the exact time in Paris when a particular moon entered or emerged from Jupiter's shadow. By knowing the local time based on the position of stars or the sun, the longitude of the astronomer's position could be established quite accurately.

For example, suppose a particular event for a moon of

Jupiter took place at 11:00 P.M. Paris time. An American astronomer in Boston observing the same event would know the exact time in Paris. At that moment a colleague would observe local star time by watching a particular star and note that it was 3:53 A.M. The local time in Boston was, therefore, 4 hours and 53 minutes (4.89 hours) later than it was in Paris. The longitude of the observatory in Boston relative to the Paris Observatory could then be determined because it takes 24 hours for Earth to make one rotation (turn through 360°). The longitude of the Boston Observatory was then 73° 23' west of the Paris Observatory because

$$(4.89/24) \times 360° = 73.38° \text{ or } 73° 23'.$$

As you may remember from Chapter 1, the prime meridian—the accepted 0° longitude line—passes through the Royal Observatory in Greenwich, England. Since Paris is 2° 20' east of Greenwich, the longitude for Boston is 71° 03' because

$$73° 23' - 2° 20' = 71° 03'.$$

Finding the latitude of a position on Earth is quite easy. The altitude of Polaris, as measured at any point north of the equator, is within half a degree of the latitude of that position, as you can see from Figure 31a. If Alkaid (the star on the end of the Big Dipper's handle) is along an imaginary horizontal line extending from Polaris, the altitude will give very nearly the exact latitude of the sighting position.

Another star that can be used to find latitude is Mintaka (δ Orion), the highest of the three stars in Orion's belt and the one farthest from Sirius, the brightest star in the sky. Mintaka lies on the celestial equator and so rises due east and sets due west. A line perpendicular to Mintaka's path across the sky is a north–south line. The latitude of a position will be very nearly equal to 90° minus the maximum altitude of Mintaka as shown in Figure 31b.

The altitude of the midday sun as determined with a sex-

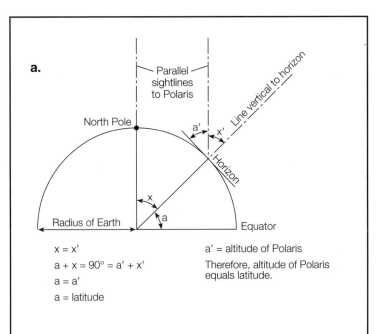

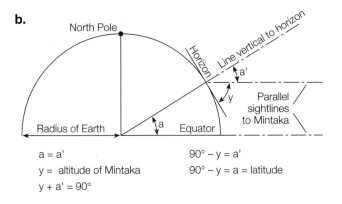

Figure 31 a. The altitude of Polaris is equal to the latitude from which the altitude is measured. **b.** Latitude can also be determined from the maximum altitude of Mintaka. (Latitude = 90° – altitude of Mintaka.)

tant can also be used to find latitude. DO NOT LOOK DI-RECTLY AT THE SUN. IT CAN DAMAGE YOUR EYES. The *Nautical Almanac* gives the sun's position (latitude and longitude) for every second of the year. At midday, the latitude of a position along that midday meridian is equal to 90° minus the sun's altitude plus the declination of the sun (its latitude). For example, if the sun's midday altitude is 43° and its declination as given in the *Nautical Almanac* is 10°, then the latitude of the observer is (90 − 43) + 10 = 57°. [See Figure 32 for the sun at maximum declination (23.5°N) and minimum declination (23.5°S).]

Finding longitude at sea was a difficult task, and in 1707 an English fleet was wrecked because of incorrect assumptions about their longitude. Seven years later, the British government established a Board of Longitude empowered to present a prize of £20,000 to whomever could build a device that would allow navigators to accurately establish their longitude. In 1763, John Harrison (1693–1776) was awarded the prize for his spring-driven No. 4 Marine Chronometer. Harrison's timepiece lost less than 2 minutes in 147 days. By setting the chronometer to match the time at longitude 0° (Greenwich Observatory), a navigator could establish longitude. If the sun at the navigator's position reached its midday maximum altitude at a time 3 hours after Greenwich noon, the navigator knew the longitude was 45° because the sun moves 15° per hour:

$$(360°/24 \text{ hr.}) = 15°/\text{hr.}$$

Today, time signals sent by radio can be transmitted around the world. A "beep" is used to establish exact times by radio. You can hear them on almost any radio station. The first such signal was sent from the Boston Navy Yard on August 9, 1905.

Using Cassini's tables and his guidance, French astronomers and scientists established benchmarks (markers that indicate the precise latitude, longitude, and altitude of

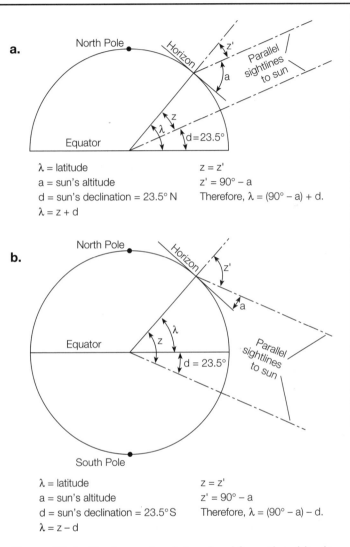

a.

North Pole

Horizon

z'

Parallel sightlines to sun

a

z

λ

d = 23.5°

Equator

λ = latitude
a = sun's altitude
d = sun's declination = 23.5° N
λ = z + d

z = z'
z' = 90° − a
Therefore, λ = (90° − a) + d.

b.

North Pole

Horizon

z'

a

λ

z

Equator

d = 23.5°

Parallel sightlines to sun

South Pole

λ = latitude
a = sun's altitude
d = sun's declination = 23.5° S
λ = z − d

z = z'
z' = 90° − a
Therefore, λ = (90° − a) − d.

Figure 32 Latitude can be determined from the altitude of the midday sun and from the sun's declination. Latitude = 90° − altitude ± declination. **a.** The sun at its maximum declination of 23.5°N. **b.** The sun at its minimum declination of 23.5°S.

that point) across France. They then proceeded to map France and found its coast to be about 80 kilometers (50 mi.) east of where earlier surveys had placed it.

Determined to extend his maps beyond France, Cassini sent missions to various parts of the world to establish benchmarks. From these forty or so positions, which are within 80 kilometers (50 mi.) of the more accurate measurements made today, he proceeded to map the world on the floor of the octagonal room in the west tower of the Paris Observatory. By 1696, Cassini had prepared world maps based on the one he had drawn on the observatory floor. These maps were beyond the dreams of Columbus, who had searched for a western route to the Orient 200 years earlier.

INVESTIGATION 22

Finding Your Latitude

Normally, you would be able to find your latitude by locating your position on a map, but to confirm your latitude, or to find it if you should lose your map, you can use a *sextant* to sight on a star or the sun. NEVER LOOK DIRECTLY AT THE SUN. IT CAN DAMAGE YOUR EYES. If you don't have a sextant, you can build a simple *astrolabe* to sight on a star. It is far less accurate, but it will give you reasonable approximations of altitudes.

On a square sheet of cardboard about 15 centimeters (6 in.) on a side, use a protractor to draw angles at 5° intervals as shown in Figure 33. Be sure the 0° and 90° lines are parallel to the sides of the square. Tape a drinking straw to the edge of the board and parallel to the 90° line. At the point where the degree lines all meet, punch a tiny hole with a needle. Then thread a thin string through the hole. Tie the end of the string behind the board to a paper clip so that it cannot slip back through the hole. Tie a metal washer or nut to the other end so that the string is under tension.

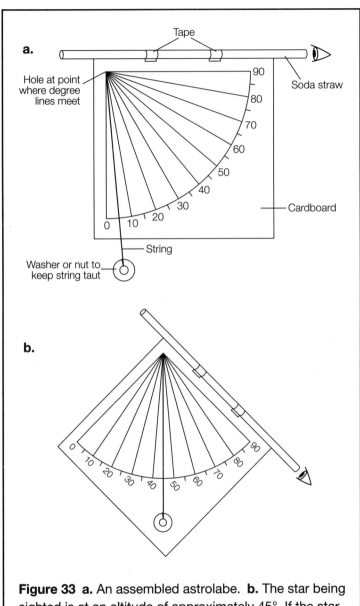

Figure 33 a. An assembled astrolabe. **b.** The star being sighted is at an altitude of approximately 45°. If the star is Polaris, the latitude is also 45°.

Notice that when you hold the astrolabe so that the 90° line is horizontal, the string lies along the 0° line, showing that the altitude of the horizon is zero. When the straw through which you will sight stars is vertical, the string lies along the 90° line, indicating a corresponding altitude. As you sight a star by looking through the straw, the string will lie along a line that indicates in degrees the altitude of the star you are sighting.

Use the astrolabe to determine the altitude of Polaris. According to your measurement, what is the latitude of the place where you are looking at Polaris? How does this compare with the latitude you can find on a map?

If possible, use the astrolabe to measure the maximum altitude of Mintaka. What is your latitude according to this measurement?

To measure the sun's midday altitude, determine the shortest shadow of a vertical stick as described in Chapter 1. The sun's declination can be found in the *Nautical Almanac* (for each second) or in *The Old Farmer's Almanac* (for each day).

DO NOT measure the sun's altitude with the astrolabe. NEVER LOOK DIRECTLY AT THE SUN. IT CAN DAMAGE YOUR EYES. Instead, use the shortest shadow of a stick at midday as you did before. Determine the ratio of the length of the stick to the length of its shadow when its shadow is shortest. If you understand trigonometry, the ratio is equal to the tangent of the sun's altitude. If you haven't had trigonometry, you can make a scaled drawing of the triangle consisting of the stick, its shadow, and the line connecting their ends. Use a protractor to measure the sun's altitude. Using that altitude and the known declination of the sun, determine your latitude. How does your calculation compare with the latitude you can find on a map?

Finding Your Longitude

With a *chronometer*, longitude can be established by measuring the time of midday in terms of *Greenwich time*. This is usually done by using a sextant to take five or more sightings on the sun beginning about 20 minutes prior to midday, and another five during the 20 minutes after midday. These readings are used to determine the exact time of midday. Suppose, for example, that midday occurs at 18 hr. 36' 0" Greenwich time. If the *Nautical Almanac* shows the longitude of the sun at 18 hr. for that day to be 92° 22', you can easily determine its longitude at 18 hr. 36' because in 36' the sun will move

$$(36/60) \times 15° = 9°.$$

Thus, the navigator's longitude is

$$92° \ 22' + 9° = 99° \ 22'.$$

For hikers, canoeists, and others traveling through the wilderness, such precise measurements of longitude are usually not possible. However, with a map and a latitude reading, a longitude reading may be possible. The latitude line can be followed east or west on a map to some important nearby feature recorded on the map. The intersection of the latitude line with that feature whose longitude can be established from the map provides a known position. A scale can then be used to determine the distance from the known position. If the known map point is latitude 48° 45', longitude 75° 00' and you are 5 kilometers (3 mi.) west of that position, then using your map scale will show that you are at longitude 75° 3.93'.

ACTIVITY 9

Mapping an Area of Land

If you have a benchmark, you can use it to draw maps of a region near the known position. Find an open area such as a playground or ball field. Assume that there is a benchmark near the center of the field, and place there the plane table you used during Activity 8.

Cover the table with a sheet of cardboard and tape it in place. Then tape a large sheet of paper to the cardboard. With a pencil, mark the center of the paper with a dot that will indicate the position of the plane table on the map. Place a compass near one corner of the paper. Draw an arrow pointing in the direction of the compass needle to show magnetic north. Have a partner steady the table while you use a pair of common pins to establish a sightline to a recognizable object such as a post, tree, or the corner of a building near one edge of the open area. Use a pencil to draw a straight line outward along this sightline. Repeat this procedure for a number of other objects around the periphery of the area. Each time, be sure the first sightline you drew is still properly oriented so that you know the plane table has not shifted. The compass will also help you to keep the map correctly oriented.

Once you have established a series of sightlines to various objects, use a measuring tape to find the distances from the plane table to each of the objects. Then choose a scale that will allow you to fit all the objects to which you have made sightlines on the paper.

After choosing an appropriate scale, draw lines connecting the points that represent objects, label the objects, and erase the sightlines you drew. Indicate the scale you used, such as 1 inch = 50 feet, in a lower corner of the drawing, and add an arrow indicating the direction of true north. To do this you will need to know the declination of the area, which can be found in a handbook of physics, maps, or other sources. You now have a map of the area. Before the sightlines are erased, it might look like the one shown in Figure 34.

To check the accuracy of your map, use it to predict the distances between some of the objects you mapped. Then measure the actual distances with a measuring tape. How do the measured distances compare with your predictions based on the map?

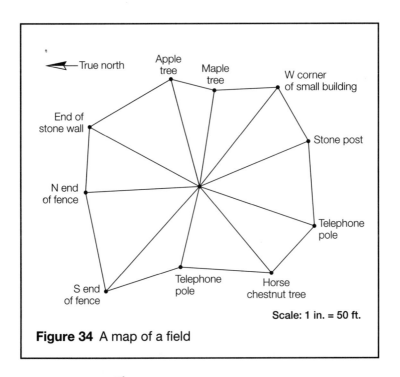

Figure 34 A map of a field

Within the figure: True north, Apple tree, Maple tree, W corner of small building, End of stone wall, Stone post, N end of fence, Telephone pole, S end of fence, Telephone pole, Horse chestnut tree, Scale: 1 in. = 50 ft.

ACTIVITY 10

Another Way to Make a Map

Another way to map an area is to make two or more sightlines to various objects from opposite ends of a base line. Prepare the plane table as you did in Activity 9. Outline the position of the compass and leave it in place. It will help in orienting the table. Choose a point near one corner of the area you wish to map. You can assume a benchmark is located at the point you choose. Put the plane table there and mark the position with a stake or some other indicator. Mark the direction of magnetic north as shown on the compass. Be sure the table is level, and keep it in position while you use two pins to make a sightline from a point near one corner of the paper to some identifiable object on the other side of the area you wish to map. Label the object and draw a sightline on the paper using a ruler and the pins. Repeat the process for a number of other objects. As you do so, check to be sure that the sightlines you drew earlier are still aligned properly.

After you have drawn a number of sightlines to objects that encompass the area you wish to map, have someone stand at a point, say 15 meters (50 ft.), toward another corner of the area to be mapped. Draw a sightline from your present position to the point where the person stands. Mark the second position and move the plane table there. Then sight back along the sightline you just made to your first position to be sure the plane table is properly oriented. These two points constitute the base line you will use in preparing the map. The sightline between these two points on the paper corresponds to the imaginary line on the ground between the two points. But how far apart should the two points be on the paper?

You will have to estimate a proper scale factor so that the map will fit on the paper. One way to do this is to sight on the object that will require the greatest change in direction relative to the original sightline. For example, if you moved left to establish a base line, sight on the object farthest to the right. If the point you chose along the base line on the paper allows the new sightline to cross the older one, your scale is satisfactory. If it does not, you will have to shrink the base line on the paper by choosing a scale with a greater ratio.

Once the plane table is properly positioned, draw new sightlines to each object you sighted from the other end of the base line. Be sure to check the table's orientation before and after you make each sightline.

When you finish, you will see that you have made a series of triangles. The base of each triangle is the same; it is the base line on the paper. The sides of the triangles are the sightlines you drew to each object from opposite ends of the base line, and the object is the apex of the individual triangles. (See Figure 35.) As a check, you could extend the base line and make a third sightline to each object.

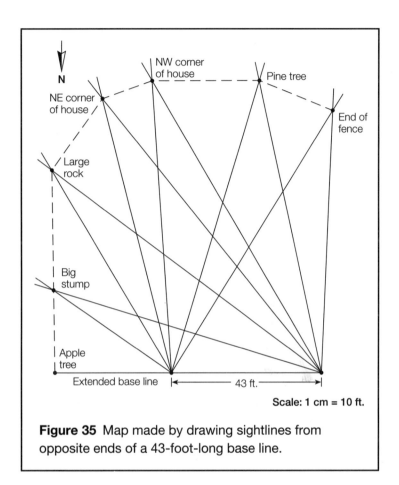

Figure 35 Map made by drawing sightlines from opposite ends of a 43-foot-long base line.

Using the scale you chose for the base line, you can use your map and a ruler to predict the distances to each object from each end of the base line and from one object to another. Then measure the distances with a measuring tape. How do the measured distances compare with your predictions based on the map?

Once you have tested your map for accuracy, you can erase the sightlines, add the scale factor, and draw an arrow indicating true north on the map.

Using a Map

Spread out a topographic map on a table. Choose a point on the map. Assume that you are at that position and you wish to travel to some other point on the map. Draw a line connecting the two points. In what direction should you move?

To find out, place the center of a transparent circular protractor or compass on the starting position you have identified on the map. The 0° (or 360°)–180° line of the protractor should

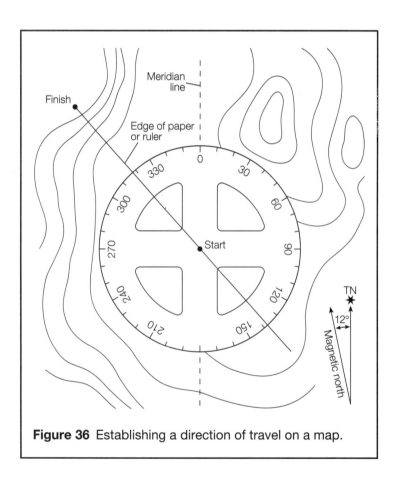

Figure 36 Establishing a direction of travel on a map.

lie parallel to a meridian, that is, along a north–south axis. Read the number of degrees where the line you drew crosses the circumference of the protractor. That reading gives you the direction you should travel.

In Figure 36, the direction of travel indicated is 316°. A reading of 0° (or 360°) would indicate that you should travel due north. A reading of 135° means you should move southeast. In what direction should you travel if the reading is 270°? If the reading is 45°? 315°? 225°? 22.5°?

If you have an orienteering compass, simply place one long edge of the compass on the map so that the edge joins the start and finish points on the map. Then turn the housing with the orienting arrow (the one that always touches 0° or 360°) so that it points north along a meridian on the map. The large direction arrow, which is parallel to the edge you used to mark the desired path along the map, will now touch the scale of degrees at the direction you should travel to reach your destination.

Based on the map's scale, how far is it from the starting point to the destination? Look at the terrain between the starting position and the destination. Is it possible to follow a straight-line path to reach the destination, or will you have to make detours around cliffs, lakes, swamps, and so on? If a straight path is not possible, how will you find your way around obstacles that may take you miles off a linear journey? How far will you have to travel to reach your destination if you take the necessary detours?

ACTIVITY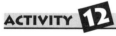

Travel by Map

It's one thing to follow a path along a map on a table; it's quite another to use a map to follow an actual path over land. To see how well you can use a map, plan a hike near your home using a topographic map of the area.

Go to the point where the hike is to begin. If you are not familiar with the territory, ask someone to accompany you. Begin by orienting the map—that is, turn the map so that north on the map matches what you see as north on the land. If you don't have a compass, you can make a rough estimate of direction by using your watch. Just point the hour hand of your watch at the sun. A point halfway between the hour hand and 12 on the watch is south. This method assumes you are on standard time. If you are on daylight saving time, use the hour line that is one less than the time on your watch to point at the sun. This is a very rough estimate of direction, but it will be sufficiently accurate to allow you to orient your map. Once the map is oriented, try to identify objects and terrain on the map that should be near your starting position.

Now begin your hike. Know where you are at all times by checking the map frequently to identify roads, streams, ponds, buildings, and other places that you can identify. But remember, some things may have changed since the map was made. Does the slope of the terrain appear to be what you would expect from the contour lines on the map? If you look at the map frequently, you should be able to follow the path you planned to hike with confidence.

ACTIVITY

Finding Landmarks

Before you set out on another hike, use the same map you used in the previous activity to identify about half a dozen landmarks found on the map. Then draw a path on the map that would take you to all the landmarks along a trail that you could walk with reasonable ease. Try to avoid steep inclines, swamps, and thick forests. Then take the map into the actual terrain, orient the map, and follow the path you indicated on the map to each of the landmarks.

Again, make sure you know the area or are accompanied

by someone who does. Estimate the distance you walk between points where you change course. Compare your estimates with the distances you would expect to walk according to the map. Study the map closely to be sure you are moving along your chosen path. If you need to change course because of changes that have taken place since the map was made, stop and use the map to develop a new and thoughtful plan of action before you begin walking again.

CHAPTER 6

Clues to Finding Your Way

Despite what you may have heard, no one has an innate sense of direction. Native Americans, as they will tell you, are no better at finding their way in the wilderness than anyone else. What backwoodsmen, experienced hikers, trail guides, and others who can find their way through uninhabited regions have in common is experience. They have learned to use maps, compasses, the sun, the stars, the wind, and a variety of other clues to guide them through unknown territory. In fact, many people who work as guides in jungles, forests, or tundra rely on familiarity with the land where they have lived all their lives. They know the landmarks and how they are positioned relative to one another. If they were placed in unfamiliar surroundings, they could easily become lost. Anyone can become lost, but it's also true that, with practice, anyone can learn to find their way through unfamiliar territory.

Polynesian sailors were able to navigate successfully from island to island, far beyond the sight of land, by using a variety of clues. They knew and remembered, from songs

124

that had been passed down from generation to generation, which star was directly above each island. They knew that clouds tend to hang over an island. They knew which birds flew close to various islands, and they could identify islands and direction by the color of the water. They could identify an island from the vegetable matter floating near it and follow its trail back to the island. They also knew the direction of prevailing winds and ocean currents.

In the Western world, prior to the arrival of the compass from the Orient, sailors steered their ships by using landmarks on or near the shore. They were afraid to lose sight of land, but when they were forced to do so, they often carried land birds on board. Periodically, they would release a bird and watch it fly higher and higher. If the bird saw land, it would fly away, and the ship would then follow the bird to land. If the bird did not detect land, it returned to the ship. Often, migrating birds led ships to land. The Portuguese found the Azores by following migrating birds at sea, and Columbus changed course and sailed to the Bahamas because he followed small land birds that were flying southwest.

Of course, in clear weather the sun provided a general east–west direction during daylight hours, and the stars were useful at night. Under cloudy skies, knowing the direction of prevailing winds was helpful. Polaris provided a means of finding latitude, and many ships used latitude sailing. They sailed north (or south) to the latitude of the port they were seeking and then sailed east (or west) by keeping Polaris on their *port* or *starboard* side.

INVESTIGATION 23

Can You Walk in a Straight Line?

You may have heard that people who are lost often walk in circles and return to the place from which they started. Perhaps this has happened to you. Even though you thought you were walking in a straight line, you actually moved along a circle.

To see if people tend to follow curved rather than straight-line paths, take your subjects to a gymnasium or a level open area. An athletic field with a light dusting of snow or a flat, hard, sandy beach are ideal. Ask one person to sight on an object directly in front of him or her. Then blindfold the individual and tell the person to walk slowly along a straight line to the object they sighted. Walk alongside that person to ensure safety, but do not influence choices of direction during the walk.

If possible, repeat the experiment several times with each subject. Do people walk in straight lines, or do they tend to follow curved paths? If they follow curved paths, do they always curve in the same direction (right or left)? Is the tendency to follow a pronouncedly curved path affected by gender? That is, are boys more likely than girls to walk in a decidedly nonlinear direction? Can you offer an explanation for the results of your experiments? Can you design experiments to test your explanations?

Avoiding Curved Paths

As you probably found in the previous investigation, people have a tendency to walk in circles. Why we do so is open to investigation. Some people claim it is because one leg always tends to be slightly longer than the other. Others argue that it is related to our dominant eye. Still others believe it is caused by an irritant force such as wind or sun. It may be because we all have a psychological proclivity for right or left.

Regardless of the cause, anyone who hikes in unfamiliar areas should be aware of the tendency and try to avoid it. If you are lost, there are various ways to ensure that you are walking along a reasonably straight-line path. The best way is to establish the direction you want to travel based on map and compass. Find a distinct landmark along or to one side of the direction you wish to travel and keep it in sight as much as possible as you walk toward it. If you plan to return along the same path, prepare back marks as you go to make your return trip an easy one. Such back marks will also allow you to return to your original site if you should become lost. Cairns, flags, sticks, or markers cut in trees can serve as back marks.

Sometimes it makes sense to make an intentional shift to the left or right of your destination. For example, if you want to reach a lake that is 3 kilometers (2 mi.) west of a mountain with a peak that you can easily distinguish, it makes sense to follow a path to the mountain and then hike west to the lake. If you try to follow a compass path directly to the lake, you might miss it.

To avoid walking in a curved path while a landmark is out of sight, you can use the wind, the sun, or shadows as guides. Keep the wind on your left cheek, for example. Keep the sun at your back and follow the direction indicated by shadows as you hike north at midday. By keeping in mind the time of day, you will find sun and shadows to be useful in following a linear path. On cloudy days, you may be able to cast a shadow by holding a shiny knife blade on a flat surface.

Although we have no sixth "directional" sense, our five senses can be useful in following a linear path. We have already mentioned sight and touch, but your ears and nose can provide useful information as well. Your ears can detect the time delay when a sound reaches one ear before the other. To eliminate that time delay, you face the sound. By facing the sound, you can walk toward the increasing intensity of sounds from surf, a waterfall, a flowing stream, the sound of wood being chopped, highway traffic, and mooing cows, barking dogs, or human conversation.

Your nose can lead you as well. Sailors can smell land, but you might be drawn by the smell of a wood fire, orange blossoms, guano, mowed hay, or a marsh at low tide.

Trees and plants are sometimes useful indicators of direction and guide you along a straight path. The growth of some species of trees such as black and white poplar, oak, beech, horse chestnut, Norway maple, and box elder is enhanced by light. As a result, their southern sides tend to show the most growth.

Pilot or resin weed (*Silphium lacinatum*) is known as "the compass plant of the prairies." It grows 1 to 2 meters (3 to 6 ft.) tall and can be found from Ohio to the Rockies and from Minnesota to Texas. Longfellow described this plant in the poem *Evangeline*. (Prairie burr-dock, *Silphium terebinthinaceum*, is a similar indicator.)

Look at this vigorous plant that lifts its head
    from the meadow,
See how its leaves are turned to the North, as true
    as a magnet;
This is the compass flower, that the finger of God
    has planted
Here in the houseless wild, to direct the traveler's
    journey
Over the sea-like, pathless, limitless waste of the
    desert.

Below the Arctic Circle, glaciers offer directional clues. Glacial debris absorbs heat, producing semicircular melt holes. The southern edges of these holes are straight, but the northern sides are rounded, revealing the melting sun's path across the sky. Sometimes, large rocks shade the ice beneath them. Because the sun melts the ice on the southern side of the rocks, pedestals form beneath the rocks. These pedestals slant southward (in the northern hemisphere). Such formations are seldom seen in the Arctic because the sun is so far south in the sky that it melts all the ice under the rocks.

In deserts, blown sand accumulates on the leeward side of obstacles. The banks of the accumulating sand slope away in a streamlined fashion, producing dunes parallel to the prevailing wind. In northern regions, snow dunes form in a similar manner, but they are generally smaller and closer together.

128

While desert birds do not provide directional clues, they can lead you to water, as can other animals such as gazelles, antelopes, bees, and hornets. On the other hand, animals such as emus and kangaroos can go without water for several days and may be found 30 to 80 kilometers (20 to 50 mi.) from water.

Lost!

You realize you're lost. It's one of life's scariest moments. The first thing to remember is, DON'T PANIC! Wherever you are lost, it helps if you have done some thinking ahead of time. In a city, arrange to meet at a particular place and time if you and those you are with should become separated. Find a police officer and show him or her the address where you are staying or where you plan to meet someone. Even if you are in a foreign country and can't communicate by speech, the officer will be able to read the address and realize that you are lost.

If you are on a wilderness hike and have done your thinking ahead of time, you are carrying a whistle. Give it three loud blows. Then stay in place and repeat the whistle blows periodically so your companions can find you. You should also have water and water-purifying tablets, a knife, matches in a waterproof bag, high-energy food, and a plastic bag that can serve as an insulating and waterproof blanket should you remain lost at nightfall.

If you are lost and you know your campsite is not far away, walk in square patterns of increasing lengths until you find it. Decide on a fixed number of paces as the length of any one of your squares. The number of paces per length will increase as your squares grow larger. Be sure the perimeters of succeeding squares are in sight of one another. A compass will help you establish right angles. If you don't have one, find an identifying landmark at the point you start your square. After making your third right-angle turn, look for the landmark as you reach the last few paces of the fourth side of the square.

Often, a river will lead to a populated area. Follow it downstream, but stay on the side away from swamps. Be careful, because in many wilderness areas a river may simply lead to another lake or pond. If you remember that the maps you had been using indicated the region was filled with lakes and ponds, following a stream is probably not a good idea.

In many regions, hills have a characteristic orientation. For example, the long axes of the Berkshires in western Massachusetts run north–south. The Appalachian Mountains are oriented along a southwest–northeast axis. Walking perpendicular to the axis of a mountain chain will bring you to lower elevations where you are more likely to find a town.

Estimating Distance

You have learned a number of ways to measure the distance you have traveled, but how can you estimate the distance to something ahead of you? One thing is certain, it's very easy to make errors in such estimates. Objects appear to be closer than they really are if you view them while looking up or down sloped ground, across water, sand, or snow, in bright light, or through very clear air. If you live in the Rocky Mountains, you may realize that the mountains appear to be closer than they really are because the air is so clear. The effect is very noticeable if you have just traveled through the Smoky Mountains, where the air is usually hazy, to the crystal-clear air of the Rockies. Objects viewed in dim light, through long corridors or canyons, over undulating ground, or against a blending background will appear farther away than they actually are.

Here are some rough guidelines for estimating distance:

- At a half mile a human looks like a post.
- At a mile, the trunks of trees are barely distinguishable.

- Chimneys and windows in buildings are just distinguishable at 2.5 miles.
- At 6 miles, large houses and towers are recognizable.
- Church steeples are visible 9 miles away.
- If the tallest trees in a region are all about the same height and you know or can measure that height, pick out a distant tree. Move your thumb, which is about 1 inch in diameter, out away from your eye until it just covers the tree so that you can no longer see the tree. Then, from the similar triangles shown in Figure 37a, you can determine the distance to the tree. For example, if your thumb blocks out the tree when held 2 feet from your eye and the tallest trees are about 40 feet, then the tree must be about 1,000 feet away because

$$24 \text{ in.}/1 \text{ in.} = X/40 \text{ ft.}; X = 24 \times 40 \text{ ft.} = 960 \text{ ft.}$$

- The distance between your eyes is about one-tenth the distance to the upright thumb of your extended arm. By

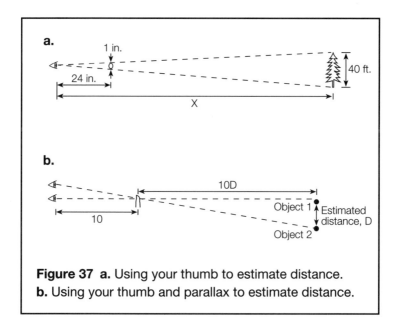

Figure 37 a. Using your thumb to estimate distance.
b. Using your thumb and parallax to estimate distance.

131

using parallax, you can make use of this anatomical fact to estimate distance. Extend your right arm and use your right eye to align your upright thumb with a distant object. Close your right eye and open your left eye. You will see your thumb appear to move to the right so that it is no longer aligned with the same distant object. Instead it is in line with some other distant object. Now, here's the difficult part. Try to estimate the distance between the two distant objects that your thumb was aligned with when you used your right eye and then your left eye. As you can see from Figure 37b, the distance from you to the objects you sighted over your thumb is ten times the estimated length separating the two distant objects.

CHAPTER 7

Map, Compass, and Orienteering

Equipped with *both* map *and* compass as well as an understanding of clues that can help you to find your way, you're ready to do some serious orienteering. That is, you are ready to move through unfamiliar surroundings from a known position to a planned destination knowing at any time during your journey almost exactly where on Earth you are.

ACTIVITY 14

Planning a Hike Using Map and Compass

Using a map of a large park or the countryside near your home, plan a hike that you will take today or in the near future. By planning your hike, you can avoid swamps, steep hills, ponds, and other obstacles that might lie along straight-line paths from starting point to destination. Choose to walk along trails, roads, and level land wherever possible. The distances may be greater than beeline paths, but travel time will probably be less and the course less demanding. If rivers and/or streams must be

These hikers are enjoying one of the beautiful views along Virginia's Skyline drive.

crossed, look for bridges on the map and adjust your route accordingly.

From the starting point on the map, place one edge of your orienteering compass's base plate along a line that connects your starting position with the first destination of your hike. The direction-of-travel arrow(s), which is (are) parallel to the edge of the base plate, will point in the direction you should walk. Turn the housing with the orienting arrow (the arrow that always touches 0° or 360°) so that it is parallel to a north–south meridian on the map. The direction-of-travel arrow(s) will now indicate the proper *geographic* direction to follow on the compass housing.

Because of magnetic declination, the geographic direction

is *not* the direction indicated by your compass. Suppose your map and compass indicate that you should travel in a direction of 100° (10° south of due east), but the map also indicates that the magnetic declination in this region is 10° west and is not changing with time. Since magnetic north is 10° west of true north, when you orient your compass in the field, north on the compass dial will be turned west (counterclockwise) by 10° relative to true north. This will add 10° to the direction indicated on the map, which is based on true north. Thus, the compass bearing you should follow is 110°.

Similarly, if the declination is 10° east, when you orient your compass, you will turn its dial east (clockwise) of true north by 10°. In this case, you should follow a bearing of 90° (magnetic east) to match the 100° direction given by map and compass.

One way to avoid these adjustments is to reorient your map so that its meridians lie along magnetic north–south lines rather than geographic ones. You can do this by extending the magnetic north arrow on the map with a ruler and pencil and then drawing a series of lines parallel to it. After you have done this, north along these new meridians will agree with magnetic north on your compass.

For each leg of your hike, use the scales on the map and compass to calculate how far you will hike. Keep a record of these distances, and take them with you as you proceed along the hike you planned. As you traverse each segment of the hike, check the distances you walk to be sure you are on a course that agrees with the map. Compare your course using both map and compass frequently as you establish and walk toward landmarks that lie along your route. If you have drawn meridians parallel to magnetic north–south on your maps, it will be very easy for you to align map north with compass north. If you are using geographic meridians, you will have to take declination into account. Place the compass over the declination arrow on the map and turn the map until the compass needle and the magnetic-north arrow on the map are parallel and point in the same direction. Rotate the compass housing until its north is parallel with geographic north on the map. Map and compass are now aligned.

PROJECT 19

Suppose you do not take a declination of 10°W into account when you plot a course but assume that magnetic north and geographic north are the same. If you plot a course to a point 1.6 kilometers (1 mi.) due north, by how many feet and in what direction will you miss your destination if you follow north as indicated on your compass?

ACTIVITY 15

Orienteering in Wilderness

Once you feel confident about finding your way with a map and compass, you are ready to use your orienteering skills in unfamiliar territory. But before you start on such a journey, there are some precautions and preparations to think about. First, and most important, find an adult experienced in wilderness travel to accompany you. Of course, you will need topographic maps of the territory, your orienteering compass, a watch, a small notebook, a knife, and pencils. Wear clothing appropriate for the season, hiking boots or shoes that can take rugged treatment (not sneakers or moccasins), heavy white socks, and a hat. On an all-day hike you will want to bring food and a canteen of water.

During your travel, be conservation minded, considerate of property owners, and ever aware of the danger of fire in dry timber or grass. If you plan an extended trip through the wilderness, either on foot or in a canoe, there are other skills you must master. These might include canoeing and camping skills; knowledge of first aid; finding and maintaining potable water; and finding, cooking, and carrying adequate and nutritious food. Do not attempt such extended trips, even if you are confident and experienced in orienteering, unless accompanied by an adult who has extensive experience in wilderness travel.

ACTIVITY **16**

Orienteering as a Sport

Orienteering races or competitions can be a lot of fun if you belong to a scout troop, a hiking, outing, camping, canoeing, biking, or mountaineering club, or some similar outdoor-related organization. If you would like to join an orienteering club in your area, you can write to

U.S. Orienteering Federation
P.O. Box 1444
Forest Park, GA 30051.

Two common orienteering competitions involve route orienteering and point orienteering. Route orienteering involves a planned route that is indicated on a map. Each participant or team receives a map and, using map and compass, proceeds to follow the map route to find landmarks along the way. At each landmark, the planners may have placed small objects that the competitors must bring back to show that they found the landmarks during their mapped hike.

In point orienteering, a series of stations are marked on a map. The competitors proceed, at intervals separated by enough time so that they cannot follow one another, to these predetermined stations where they are checked by a judge or bring back some identifiable marker. Each participant or team decides on the best path to follow to reach the station. In some races, only one station is indicated at the start. The location of the second station is found at the site of the first station and so on until the final destination is reached. For example, at station 3, participants might find the location of station 4. The location given might read, "Station 4 is 5,000 feet away, at 145° from the bridge crossing the stream that runs from Salmon Creek to South Fork River."

Together with a small group of orienteering enthusiasts, you could prepare instructions and rules for an orienteering competition. At the same time, another group could prepare a program in which you might compete. If you like orienteering, you will probably enjoy preparing maps and instructions for route or point orienteering and inventing ingenious programs of your own.

CHAPTER 8

Modern Methods of Finding Where on Earth You Are

Since the beginning of the space age nearly 40 years ago, giant strides in technology have provided a wide variety of tools that enable us to determine where on Earth we are with an accuracy never dreamed of half a century ago. On a recent ocean cruise, the crew asked the passengers to guess the distance the ship had traveled since leaving port. Because the ship's speed is reported several times each day, many of the passengers used dead reckoning to calculate the distance that the ship had traveled. Most of them came within 100 nautical miles of the actual distance traveled, but the winner of the contest was within 1 mile of the actual distance. In the second such contest held 2 days later, *Global Positioning Systems* (*GPS*), the navigational device that had enabled the winner of the first contest to obtain such an accurate result, were not allowed. You'll learn more about the GPS later in this chapter, but first let's take a look at some other navigational systems.

Interference of Radio Waves

When two radio towers transmit the same signal (wavelength), they produce what is called an interference pattern. A similar pattern is produced on a smaller scale when two small spheres moving up and down at the ends of two rods generate water waves. Where the crests of waves from one source meet the troughs of waves from the second source and vice versa, the waves cancel one another out and a thin motionless region extends outward from between the two sources. Such a line is called a nodal line, and the number of nodal lines depends on the wavelength and the distance between the two wave sources.

When radio waves are generated on either side of a runway at an airport, and the waves at one source are delayed by half a wavelength relative to the other, a nodal line will extend outward along a line that bisects the line between the two sources. A plane that follows such a nodal line by maintaining silence on a radio tuned to the frequency of the waves generated will be led to the airport runway.

Loran

Loran is an acronym for Long-Range Navigation. Designed to help ships navigate along coastal waters, this device consists of a series of radio transmitters sending out synchronized signals. Receivers on ships measure the time difference between the signals received from two different stations. Like all radio waves, these signals travel at the speed of light (300,000 km/s or 186,000 mi./s). Nevertheless, the receivers can detect time differences as short as 0.1 microsecond (1.0×10^{-7} s). In such a short time, the signal still travels a distance that can easily be calculated:

$$(3.0 \times 10^5 \text{ km/s}) \times (1.0 \times 10^{-7} \text{ s}) = 3.0 \times 10^{-2} \text{ km or } 30 \text{ m.}$$

Two point sources of waves produce the interference pattern
shown here. On the upper right hand side of the photo, you
can see three nodal lines quite clearly.

Consequently, a ship can determine its position to within 30 meters (100 ft.).

A computer connected to the receiver is programmed to respond to the time delay between these signals and other signals that identify the position of the two transmitters. Using these data, the computer displays the ship's position as a longitude and a latitude, which is easily found on a chart of the region. With position known, it is an easy matter to plot a course to a desired destination. Then, using the ship's speed, a time of arrival can be predicted.

PROJECT 20

At 9:30 A.M., a ship is found to be at a position 150 nautical miles from its destination. Its cruising speed is 12 knots. What is its predicted time of arrival?

Global Positioning System (GPS)

The United States Defense Department has spent $10 billion on a GPS that allows military navigators to determine their position (longitude and latitude to within about 10 meters). The system consists of 24 NAVSTAR satellites in orbits about the Earth's poles at altitudes of more than 16,000 kilometers (10,000 mi.). These satellites are equipped with atomic clocks that transmit radio signals at precise moments in time. Special radio receivers equipped with computers are programmed to compare the time the signal was sent with the time it is received. With this information, the distance of the receiver from the satellite can be established because the radio signal travels at the speed of light (300,000 km/s or 186,000 mi./s).

One such signal indicates only how far the receiver is from the satellite. On a flat surface, it could be anywhere along a circle centered on S_1 as shown in Figure 38. But an-

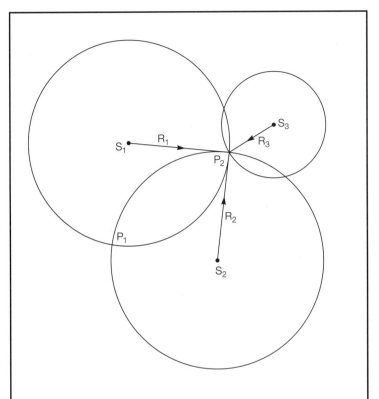

Figure 38 Satellites S_1, S_2, and S_3 emit signals at precise moments of time. The circumferences of the circles mark the positions of the signals after a known interval on a flat surface. Since all the signals travel at the speed of light, the time for the signals to reach a receiver is proportional to the distance of the receiver from each satellite. The point where the three signals (circles) intersect (P_2) is the position of the receiver. It is R_1 from S_1, R_2 from S_2, and R_3 from S_3. Circles are shown rather than spheres because it is difficult to show spheres in two-dimensional drawings, but the principle is the same.

other signal can be received from a second satellite, S_2. This establishes a second circle on which the receiver could be located. The receiver must be located at one of the two points, P_1 or P_2, where the two circles intersect. A third signal from yet another satellite, S_3, will define the ship's position because three circles about S_1, S_2, and S_3 can intersect at only one point. In Figure 38, P_2 is that point.

In the real three-dimensional world, the signal from the satellite at any moment in time is at the surface of an imaginary sphere centered on the satellite, and four satellite signals are used by GPS receivers. Suppose your GPS receiver finds that you are distance d_1 from one satellite, distance d_2 from a second satellite, and d_3 from a third. This places you at the intersection of three separate and different spheres. Now, two spheres can intersect in, at most, a circle; three spheres can meet in at most two points—the points where the third sphere touches that circle. In reality, one of those two points would be recognized as false because it would be beyond the Earth's surface or beneath it. A fourth signal from a fourth satellite, which would eliminate that spurious position, is used primarily to synchronize the computer's timer with the atomic clocks on the satellites.

Because the time intervals can be measured to tenths of microseconds (1.0×10^{-7} s) or better, your position can be determined very accurately by the receiver's computer—to within a few meters of the true location. The longitude and latitude are displayed on a screen.

PROJECT 21

Given that time can be measured to a tenth of a microsecond (1.0×10^{-7} s) using GPS and that the speed of light is 300 million meters per second (3.0×10^8 m/s), show that a position can be established to within 30 meters.

GPS was designed to guide troops and weapons and played a significant part in routing the Iraqi army during the 1991 Gulf War. Because the military still controls the NAVSTAR satellites, they transmit two types of signals. One is coded and highly precise; the second is degraded for civilian use and enables users to establish position to within about 30 meters (100 ft). For a canoeist lost in the wilderness, 30 meters (1.0 seconds of longitude and latitude) is more than sufficient to locate his or her position on a map. It is a distance equivalent to the separation of homes on small lots or one-third the length of a football field.

In the early part of the 1900s, following the Wright brothers' initial flights, airplane pilots navigated by observing landmarks. Then, in 1925, landing fields were lighted and emergency fields were established at 40-kilometer (25-mi.) intervals with beacons at 16-kilometer (10-mi.) intervals. The light beacons were gradually replaced by radio beacons because radio waves, unlike light waves, are not reflected or absorbed by fog or clouds. In the last decade, GPS has had a profound effect on airlines. Equipment has been developed that can keep pilots within 3 meters (10 ft.) of the glide slope during landings. Such equipment will allow even small airports to remain open under all weather conditions. GPS is also used by most large oceangoing vessels, and a chain of radio transmitters built along the American coastline by the United States Coast Guard will allow ships' receivers to pinpoint their position to within 5 meters (16 ft.) at distances of up to 240 kilometers (150 miles).

There are GPS receivers designed for cars and trucks. Although still in the experimental stage, eventually cars will have a GPS system coupled with a map on the dashboard that will give the driver the vehicle's location. When the driver enters a destination, the onboard computer will map the best route to follow.

Even hikers, canoeists, hunters, fishing enthusiasts, and

A hand-held GPS receiver can be very useful to hikers, canoeists, and campers who enjoy wilderness adventure.

explorers can now use GPS to find their position on the surface of the Earth. Hand-held receivers about the size of a small telephone can be purchased for about $200. (Some say that the price will eventually fall to $50.) The device, which can pick up the NAVSTAR satellites' signals, will not only show your present longitude and latitude on a small screen, it will allow you to store the positions of various landmarks in its memory so that you have a record of the return path you should follow.

It will even guide you along a path from your present position to your destination. It does not, however, work well under the heavy tree cover of a forest. It needs to be able to "see" its satellites; that is, it has to be able to receive their signals, and these signals can sometimes be obscured. Ordinary radio waves have a long wavelength. Such waves easily diffract (spread around) ordinary objects such as trees and buildings. However, the wavelengths of the radio signals from NAVSTAR satellites are too small to diffract around buildings or dense forest. Consequently, the use of GPS requires a reasonably clear view of the sky and the horizon where the satellites are located.

GPS makes older methods of navigation obsolete, and, to a large extent, it removes much of the challenge of finding your way through unknown regions. With a hand-held GPS receiver, you can easily answer the question, "Where on Earth am I?" All you have to do is turn on the receiver, wait a few seconds for it to find the satellites it needs, and then read the screen.

Appendix

Where to Buy Maps

Maps of all kinds may be obtained from a local map distributor (see the Yellow Pages of your telephone book). To obtain topographic maps of an area in the United States, write to:

Map Information Office
United States Geological Survey
Washington, DC 20242.

Request a *Topographic Map Index Circular* of the state you plan to explore as well as the Geological Survey booklet on *Topographic Maps* and decide what maps you need. For maps EAST of the Mississippi River, send your order and money to:

Branch of Distribution
U.S. Geological Survey

1200 South Eads Street
Arlington, VA 22202.

For maps WEST of the Mississippi, write to:

Branch of Distribution
U.S. Geological Survey
Federal Center
Denver, CO 80225.

For Canadian topographic maps, write to:

Map Distribution Office
Dept. of Energy, Mines, and Resources
615 Booth Street
Ottawa, Ontario K1A OE9
Canada.

You can probably obtain maps faster, but at a slightly higher cost, from your state geological survey office. Other sources of maps include the United States Forest Service, the United States National Park Service, your state's Department of Conservation, and your local Chamber of Commerce or Surveying Office. Local waterway maps can be obtained from a regional office of the United States Army Corps of Engineers.

Glossary

agonic line—a line of positions along which compass needles point toward true north (declination = 0°).

astrolabe—a device that can be used to observe and calculate the positions of celestial bodies.

astronomical unit (AU)—the distance of the Earth from the sun (approximately 150,000,000 kilometers or 93 million miles). Astronomers often use the AU as a unit of distance.

chronometer—a very precise clock or watch. By setting a chronometer to match the time at longitude 0° (Greenwich Observatory), one can establish longitude. For example, if the sun at the observer's position reaches its midday maximum altitude at 3 hours after Greenwich noon, the longitude of that location is 45° because the sun moves 15° per hour.

Coriolis force—a fictitious force caused by Earth's rotation. For example, air masses moving north or south across the Earth's Northern Hemisphere appear to be deflected to the right of their paths, as if a force is pushing them.

dead reckoning—obtaining one's approximate position by using the product of the velocity and the time to determine displacement from a previously known position.

geocentric—Earth centered.

Global Positioning System (GPS)—a system consisting of 24 NAVSTAR satellites in orbit about the Earth's poles. Equipped with atomic clocks, the satellites transmit radio signals that allow navigators on Earth's surface to determine their position (longitude and latitude) to within a few meters.

gravitational field—a gravitational force exerted on a unit mass at all points surrounding a large mass, such as Earth. Earth's gravitational field can be represented by lines with arrowheads that point toward the Earth's center. The direction of these lines (the number passing through a unit area) indicates the strength of the field.

great circle—a circle on the surface of a sphere whose center lies at the center of the sphere. Such a circle divides the globe into two equal hemispheres. The arc of the great circle is always the shortest distance between two points on a sphere.

Greenwich time—the time at the Prime Meridian (0° longitude), which passes through Greenwich, England.

heliocentric—sun-centered. The solar system is heliocentric because all of the planets orbit the sun.

horizon—the "apparent horizon" is the intersection of an observer's Earth and sky. The "sensible horizon" is the circular intersection of a plane tangent to Earth, at the location of the observer, with the celestial sphere.

isogonic line—a line of positions along which compass needles have the same declination.

latitude—the angular distance north or south of the equator. Latitudinal lines 1° apart are separated by 60 nautical miles (111 km or 69 mi.) because 1 nautical mile was designed to be 1 minute of arc along the Earth's surface.

longitude—the angular distance east or west of the Prime Meridian, an imaginary line extending from the North Pole and running due south along the Earth's surface to the South Pole. Longitudinal lines 1° apart are separated by 60 nautical miles (111 km or 69 mi.) at the equator, but the distance gradually shrinks until it reaches zero when the lines meet at the poles.

magnetic declination—the difference in angle between the reading on a magnetic compass and true or geographic north.

meridian—a great circle on the Earth's surface that passes through the North and South Poles. Meridians are used to measure longitude. The Prime Meridian, which passes through Greenwich, England, has been established as 0° longitude.

orienteering compass—a compass designed to make it easier to find a direction of travel.

pace—the distance between the point where the heel of one foot is raised to the point where the same heel is put down again following a step by the other foot. A normal pace is about 1.5 meters (5 ft.) long.

parallax—an apparent change in the direction of an object relative to a more distant object. The apparent change in the direction of the object is caused by a change in the observer's position.

period—the time it takes to make one orbit of the sun.

port—the left-hand side of a ship as one faces the bow.

Prime Meridian—the point arbitrarily chosen as 0° longitude. It passes through Greenwich, England.

proper motion—a consistent angular motion of a star in a particular direction, which may amount to several seconds of arc per year, along the celestial sphere. Because of their proximity, nearer stars generally have larger proper motions than more distant stars.

protractor—an instrument used to measure and construct angles.

sightline/line of sight—an imaginary straight line extending from a viewer's eye to the object being observed.

solenoid—a cylindrical coil of wire with a hollow core. When an electric current flows through the coil, a magnetic field is created. (A solenoid's magnetic field is similar to the magnetic field of a bar magnet.)

starboard—the right-hand side of a ship as one faces the bow.

subtend—to be opposite to and delimit. For example, the side of a triangle subtends the opposite angle. The moon subtends about half a degree along the celestial sphere relative to an observer's eye.

topographic map—a map that shows the character, natural features, and land configuration. It also has contour lines that provide information about altitude.

Tropic of Cancer—a line of latitude 23.5° north of the equator. It marks the sun's northernmost apparent path across the Earth.

Tropic of Capricorn—a line of latitude 23.5° south of the equator. It marks the sun's southernmost apparent path across the Earth.

For Further Reading

"Finding the Future," *The Economist*. Nov. 6, 1993, p. 115.

Gatty, Harold. *Nature Is Your Guide: How to Find Your Way on Land and Sea*. New York: Penguin, 1979.

Jacobson, Cliff. *The New Wilderness Canoeing & Camping*. Merrillville, Indiana: ICS Books, 1986.

McVey, Vicki. *The Sierra Club Wayfinding Book*. Boston: Little, Brown, 1988.

Melton, Luke. *Piloting with Electronics*. Camden, Maine: International Marine Publishing Company, 1987.

Mitani, Sam. "GPS and the No-Longer-Lost Generation," *Road and Track*. July 1994.

Mooers, Robert L. Jr. *Finding Your Way in the Outdoors*. New York: E. P. Dutton, 1972.

Morrison, Philip, and Phylis Morrison. *The Ring of Truth: An Inquiry into How We Know What We Know*. New York: Random House, 1987.

Index

Nimbers in *italics* indicate illustrations.

Agonic line, 79, *81*
Altitude, finding, 112-114
Angular measurements, 20-26
Aristotle, 15
Astrolabe, 112-114, *113*
Astronomical unit (AU), 43
  value of, 51

Bearing, finding, 88-90
Brahe, Tycho, 41, 51

Cassini, Jean Dominique, 50-51
  map making, 107-108, 110-111
Celestial sphere, 20, *21*
  angular distances, 20-26

Chronometer, 114
Circles
  great circles, 18, 73-74
  walking in, 125-126
Circumference
  of earth, 17, 28-31
  and measuring wheels, 68-70
Columbus, 79
Compass, 76-77. *See also* Orienteering compass
  how to make one, 84-85, *85*
  use to walk triangle, 90-92
Constellations, 26-27, *27*
  names of, 37
Contour lines, 99
  mapping, 100-106

Copernican view, 36–37, 46–48
  acceptance of, 41–42
  endorsed by Galileo, 38–39
Copernicus, Nicolas, 36–37, 38
  radius of Mercury's orbit, 45
Coriolis forces, 56–58
Curvature of the Earth, 32–33

Dead reckoning, 71–73
Declination, 21
Diameter
  of celestial sphere, 20
  of Earth, 16–17, 28–31
  of Earth's orbit, 40
Direction
  guides to, 126–129
  no innate sense of, 124
  and orienteering compass, 88–89
  travel by map, 120–123, *120*
Distance
  estimating, 130–132, *131*
  to horizon, 32–34, *33*
  from Mars, 50–51
  to planets, 42–45
Distance, measure using
  dead reckoning, 71–73
  pacing, 70–71
  parallax, 61–65, *63, 64*
  range finder, 66–68, *67*
  similar triangles, 65–66, *65*
  wheels, 68–70, *69*

Earth
  as center of universe, 10
  curvature of, 32–33
  elliptical orbit, *42*
  imaginary grid, 18–20
  measure diameter, 16–17, 28–31
  measure girth, 28–31
  shape of, 13–15, *14*
Electricity and magnetism, 83–84
Eratosthenes, 16–17, 18
Eyes, which is dominant, 28

Foucault, Jean, 52–54
Foucault pendulum, 52–54, *53*
  build a model, 55–56, *55*

Galileo, 38–39
  forced to recant, 41
  observations of Venus, 46, 48
  and parallax, 40
Geocentric universe, 37, *49*
  model of, 37–38
Geographic direction, 134–135
Gilbert, William, 77–78
Glaciers, directional clue, 128
Global Positioning System

(GPS), 142-147, *143, 146*
cost of, 147
Gravitational field, 76, 77
Great circles, 18, 73-74

Harrison, John, 110
Heliocentric solar system, 37
  evidence of, 52-54, 56-58
  model of, 37
  observations of Venus, 48, *49*
Hemispheres, 18-20
Hiking, 92-95, 133-136
Hills, 102-107, *103, 104, 106*
Horizon, 32-34, *33*

Interference pattern, 140, *141*
Isogonic line, 79, *80*

Jupiter
  moons, 39, 107-108
  period, 50

Kepler, Johannes, 41-42

Landmarks, finding, 122-123
Latitude, 18, *19*
  find it, 108-114, *109, 111*
  latitude sailing, 125
  on topographic maps, 97
Longitude, *19*
  as great circles, 73-74
  finding it, 110, 114-115

on celestial sphere, 21
on topographic maps, 97, 99
Loran (Long-Range Navigation), 140, 142
Lost, what to do, 129-130

Magnetic declination, 79, *80, 81*
  geographic direction, 134-135
  how to find it, 82-83, *82*
Magnetic fields, 75-76, *78*
  and electricity, 83-84, *83*
Magnets
  bar magnets, 76, 77, 79
  how to make one, 84-85
  and magnetic fields, 75-76
Mapping
  area of land, 115-119, *117, 119*
  hills, 102-105, *103, 104*
  a model terrain, 100-101
  the world, 107-112
Maps, 96. *See also* Topographic maps
  mental maps, 9
  road maps, 9-10
  using, 120-123
  where to buy, 149-150
Mars, distance from, 50-51
Meridians, 18-20
Movement, 35-36
  of celestial bodies, 35-38
  and Coriolis forces, 56-58
  proper motion of stars, 52

Movement (*Continued*)
  relative motion, 36

Navigation
  before the compass, 125
  GPS, 142-147, *143*, *146*
  interference pattern, 140,
    142
  Loran, 140, 142
  mental maps, 9
  Polynesian sailors, 124–
    125
Newton, Isaac, 41, 52

Obstacles, 93-94, *94*
Orbits,
  of Earth, *42*
  orbital radii, 42-45, *44*,
    48-51, *50*
  of planets, 41
Orienteering, 136-138
Orienteering compass, 85–
    88, *86*, *87*
  cost of, 85
  deal with obstacles, 93-94,
    94
  find bearings, 88
  follow bearings, 89
  hiking, 92-95, *94*
  reading declination, 83
  use to return, 89-90
  use with a map, 121
  walk a triangle, 90-92, *91*

Pacing, 70-71

Parallax, 39-40
  among stars, 51-52
  use to measure distance,
    61-65
Periods, 43, 50
  relationship to radius, 41
Planets
  elliptical orbits, 41, *42*
  how far away are they?,
    42-45
  measure radius of, 48-51
  "wanderers", 35-36
Polaris, the North Star,
  altitude, *109*
  and latitude sailing, 125
  location of, 24, *25*
Polo, Marco, 76
Prime Meridian, 19
Pythagorean equation, 32
Ptolemy, 48

Radii of planets, 48-51
Radio waves and interfer-
    ence, 140
Range finders, 66-68, *67*
Relative motion, 36
Richer, Jean, 50
Right ascension, *21*
Rotation
  and atmosphere, 39
  and celestial bodies, 36-39
  evidence of, 52-54, 56-58

Shadows, 15-16
  and shape of earth, 15

using to measure, 16-17, 28-31

Shapes
of earth, 13-15, *14*
and shadows, 15-16

Shortest routes, 73-74

Sightlines
establish with dominant eye, 28
use in making maps, 115-119

Stars
distance to nearest, 20
and parallax, 40, 51-52
proper motion of, 52

Straight lines, walking, 125-126

Telescope, 48, 51-52

Topographic maps, 97-100, *98*
hiking, 133-136
hills, 102-107, *103, 104, 106*

model terrain, 100-101, *101*

Trees, as guides, 127-128

Triangles
measure with, 65-66, *65*
walk one, 90-92

Venus
changing, 46-48, *47, 49*
radius of the orbit, 42-45
when it is visible, 43, 45

Visibility and horizon, 32

Walking in circles, 125-126
avoiding it, 126-129

"Wanderers", 35-36

Wheels, measuring with, 68-70, *69*

Wilderness, travel in, 136-137

World, mapping, 107-112

About the Author

Robert Gardner taught physical science, physics, chemistry, and biology for more than 30 years at the Salisbury School in Salisbury, Connecticut, prior to his retirement. A *School and Library Journal* reviewer has called him "the master of the science experiment book," and his book have won numerous awards and citations. Mr.Gardner, who has written more than fifty science books for children and young adults, no lives on Cape Cod in Massachusetts with his wife, Natalie.